MW00814754

Historic Church Serves Big City

In tribute to your and
Anna's work as
members of the Order
of the Holy Family —

Phyllis

Historic Church Serves Big City

St. Andrew's Episcopal Church
Provides Sanctuary in the City

PHYLLIS KESTER

Foreword by William Winterrowd

RESOURCE *Publications* · Eugene, Oregon

HISTORIC CHURCH SERVES BIG CITY
St. Andrew's Episcopal Church Provides Sanctuary in the City

Resource Publications
An Imprint of Wipf and Stock Publishers
199 W. 8th Ave., Suite 3
Eugene, OR 97401

www.wipfandstock.com

HARDCOVER ISBN: 978-1-7252-6027-6

Historic Church Serves Big City is dedicated to five Episcopal clergy whose vision and inspiration charted the course of history of the little church on the edge of downtown, St. Andrew's Episcopal Church, to serve the common good of Denver, Colorado. Each clergy is listed with their dates of service in Denver.

The Right Reverend John Franklin Spalding, 1874–1902

The Reverend Neil Stanley, 1920–1942

The Reverend Jon Marr Stark, 1969–1984

The Reverend Kenneth Near, 1986–1991

The Reverend Constance Delzell, 1991–2007

Contents

Foreword

By the Right Reverend William Winterrowd, Colorado Episcopal Bishop, 1991–2003

Phyllis Kester identifies her 150-year history of St. Andrew's Episcopal Church by using a powerful image that reflects the unique identity of the parish. She says, "St. Andrew's continues to wrestle with the question of how to provide sanctuary in the city." Ordinarily the word "sanctuary" describes the area of the church building where sacred worship takes place. This image of St. Andrew's as sanctuary in the city is a radical departure from traditional theology.

Kester refers to the ministry of St. Andrew's as countercultural. Welcoming gays to participate in the life of the parish often counters church and society. When mainline churches were in denial and offered nothing to assist AIDS victims, St. Andrew's became a center of pastoral care for the victims of AIDS in the 1980s, offering sanctuary in the city.

An essential component of sanctuary is hospitality to strangers. The biblical imperative to welcome the stranger is a common thread of St. Andrew's history, as seen in the story of Richie. Twelve-year-old Richie ran away from his home in Chicago in 1969. He was taken in by the brothers of St. Andrew's Abbey, who gave him gentle lovingkindness that enabled him to get his life back together.

In the beginning of Scripture (Genesis 18), Abraham, by the oaks of Mamre, welcomed three strange men into his abode. In the

New Testament, Jesus appears to two of the disciples on the road to Emmaus (Luke 14:13.) Without recognizing Jesus, one of the disciples invites him to have dinner with them. When we welcome the stranger, we inevitably encounter "the Divine." As Scripture reveals in Matthew 18:20, "Where two or three gather together in my name, I am there in their midst."

A constant thread in St. Andrew's sanctuary in the city has been its ministry to children. Throughout twentieth-century parish history, it clearly heard Jesus' admonition in Matthew 9:14, "Let the little children come to me and do not stop them, for it is to such as these that the Kingdom of Heaven belongs." Kester points out that these words are illustrated in the central panel of the reredos above the altar at St. Andrew's. Its long ministry to children culminated with the Children's Arts and Learning Center under Rector Connie Delzell's leadership. It was my privilege to be present when the Center's St. Cecilia Singers of fifty children performed at our National Cathedral in Washington, DC. The parish ministry to children continued to thrive in the founding of its second Episcopal school in Denver, St. Elizabeth's School, established in 2007.

The word "sanctuary" is derived from the Latin word *sacra*, which means "sacred." With a continuum of sacred and secular, our world is dominated by what it considers secular. What the world sees as sacred is limited to sacerdotal rituals that take place in church sanctuaries. It leaves very little for what it narrowly defines as trivial. St. Andrew's, with its mission to be the sanctuary for the city, sees the proper paradigm as the sacred and the profane. What makes St. Andrew's identity as sanctuary in the city so powerful is that we live in a very profane world. Any serious study of the life of Jesus reflects a ministry dominated by caring for people who live in a world filled with the sick, the poor, the addicted, and the abused. In their city of Denver, St. Andrew's parishioners hear the voice of Jesus saying in Matthew 25:45, "Inasmuch as you have done it to one of the least of these you have done it unto me."

Because many of our churches are content with the old paradigm, their ministries are mostly irrelevant or nonexistent. Diana Butler Bass says in her book *Grounded*, "that is why the most consequential question of our times is: Where is God? Some stubbornly maintain that a distant God sits on his heavenly throne watching all these things. Such a divinity looks increasingly absurd." This is likely why many of our churches are like museums of the past with very few people in ministry.

Throughout her book, Kester shows how the life of St. Andrew's has been deeply impacted by its clergy leaders. Because they shared a unique vision for the parish, she says, "their ministries are the adventures of pioneering ministries." Even in bad times when the resources were minimal and the survival of St. Andrew's was in doubt, they never gave up on their vision. From Bishop Spalding to the Rev. Connie Delzell, they seem to have known Proverbs 29:18, "Where there is no vision, the people do perish." So the vision of St Andrew's as sanctuary in the city goes forward.

Acknowledgments

Archeological digging through time (historical research) starts with lots of mystery. It bumps into strange twists and turns. Yet the companions-on-the-way are nuggets of gold.

At the beginning of this "dig" were parish historians at St. Andrew's Episcopal Church in Denver. Judith James invited me to research the life of Fr. Neil Stanley. Jay Thomas joined the mystery sleuthing. Jay also proposed a historical book to celebrate the parish sesquicentennial in 2024. Brock Erickson collaborated on a historical map of the parish block on Glenarm Place. Ralph Valentine devoted six years of collegial teamwork and unfailing support.

Beyond the parish circle, local archivists led further into the dusty past. I am forever indebted to St. John's Cathedral archivists Nancy Woodward and Linda Hargrave, the Colorado Episcopal diocese archivist Kay Ward, and St. Anne's Episcopal School historical conservationists Merrie Need and Lori Frank.

Providing headlamps into the dark pathways, Denver Public Library librarians James Jeffrey, Abby Hoverstock, and Frank Wilmot were invaluable. Countless other DPL librarians offered beams of light. St. John's Cathedral librarian, Ann Jones, gave non-stop assistance.

Specialists along the way opened up new direction. Graphic designer Dwane Cohen designed a historic map of the 2000 block of Glenarm Place. Communication director of the Colorado

Acknowledgments

Episcopal Diocese Mike Orr published an article in the *Colorado Episcopalian* to give a preview of my historical quest. Likewise, David Skidmore of *The Historiographer* reprinted my story for the National Episcopal Historians and Archivists.

Encouragement and inspiration came throughout my research and writing adventure from my lifelong friend, Norma Cook Everist. She was my North Star.

Consistent enlightenment came from my daughter, Jill Locantore, and my son-in-law, Frank Locantore, who offered perpetual interpretation of my computer mysteries. Without their computer technology expertise, this story would never have seen the light of day.

Priceless consultants completed the pantheon of archeological discovery. Ethan Anthony, principal architect, Cram and Ferguson Architects, Concord, Massachusetts; Barbara Benedict, reporter/editor, *Colorado Episcopalian*, 1963–1993; Martha Bollenbacher, parishioner, St. Andrew's Episcopal Church, 1980s-present; Brother Francis, Order of the Holy Family, 1972–1980; the Rev. Sally Brown, deacon, St. Andrew's Episcopal Church, 1995–2009 ; the Rev. Connie Delzell, rector, St. Andrew's Episcopal Church, 1991–2007; Brother Ron Fox, assistant to the president, Bexley Seabury Seminary, Chicago; the Rt. Rev. William C. Frey, Episcopal bishop of Colorado, 1973–1990; Gertie, Melanie, and Newell Grant, grandchildren of William West Grant II, Denver; Michael Knudsen, administrative assistant, Bethany House, 1995–2000; Timothy Krueger, choirmaster, St. Andrew's Episcopal Church, 1995–present; the late Rev. Hal Lycett, 1959 Nashota House Seminary classmate of Abbot Jon Marr Stark; Ken Miller, historical conservationist, Denver; Aaron Moody, Skyline Stained Glass, Denver; the Rev. Ken Near, rector, St. Andrew's Episcopal Church, 1986–1991; the Rev. Richard Palmer, 1959 Nashota House Seminary classmate of Abbot Jon Marr Stark; Richie Pardo, young guest of the Order of the Holy Family, 1969; Candy Porter, historian, Charles Winfred Douglas Homestead, Evergreen, Colorado; Christopher Pote, seminary archivist, Virginia Theological Seminary, Alexandria, Virginia; Dr. Gregory Robbins, chair, Religious Studies, University of Denver; Marge Ruby, wife of organist

Acknowledgments

Hank Ruby at St. Andrew's Episcopal Church, intermittently from 1948–1970; Micah Saxton, head librarian, Iliff School of Theology, Denver; the Rev. Jon Marr Stark, rector, St. Andrew's Episcopal Church, abbot of St. Andrew's Abbey, 1969–1984; Jane Watkins, Watkins Stained Glass Studio, Denver; the Rev. John Wengrovious, historian, Colorado Episcopal Church, Golden, Colorado; the late Rev. Bert Womack, canon to the ordinary during Bishop Frey's tenure, 1973–1990; the Rev. Stephen Zimmerman, historian, Anglican/Episcopal Church, Cape Coral, Florida.

1

Kaleidoscope of Visions

NINETEENTH-CENTURY VISION FOR COLORADO EPISCOPAL CHURCH

As the United States embarked on western expansion in the nineteenth century, so did churches. While the U.S. government initiated exploratory expeditions, the Episcopal Church sent missionary bishops to explore western territories. Some half-dozen Episcopal missionary bishops took turns surveying western regions and establishing little churches in the Colorado territory and adjacent lands.

In February 1874, the last of the Episcopal missionary bishops arrived in Denver and began an aggressive purchase of real estate. The Rt. Rev. John Franklin Spalding used his land purchases to begin planting seeds of his vision for Episcopal churches, schools, and hospitals.

The Rt. Rev. John Franklin Spalding served as missionary bishop
of Colorado and Wyoming, 1874–1887. He then served as
first diocesan bishop, 1887–1902.

One such land purchase was the 2000 block of Glenarm Place,
which was then known as Lincoln Street. By the 1880s, this seminal
land purchase was home to the first Episcopal cathedral in Colorado
along with an Episcopal school for boys and an Episcopal seminary.
In the 1890s, St. Luke's Episcopal Hospital School of Nursing also
occupied space on the Cathedral Close—the name given to this
virgin block on Glenarm Place.

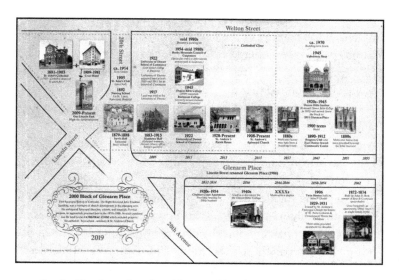

Seminal land purchase by Bishop Spalding became the home of the
Cathedral Close in the 1880s and 1890s. In 1908, Trinity Memorial Church
was built on the northern edge of the Cathedral Close.

NINETEENTH-CENTURY VISION
FOR NEW DENVER PARISH

Even before Bishop Spalding established the Cathedral Close property with its Episcopal institutions, he oversaw the establishment
of a brand-new parish on the growing eastern edge of Denver,
Colorado. In March 1874, the bishop presided at the laying of the
cornerstone. In June 1874, Bishop Spalding formally opened Trinity Memorial Chapel. It was the second Episcopal church in Denver,
following St. John's Church in the Wilderness founded in 1860. The
newly formed mission church, Trinity Memorial Chapel, provided
the office for Bishop Spalding for the next several years.

The brand-new parish was named in honor of a previous missionary bishop by the name of George Maxwell Randall. Bishop
Randall served for seven years, from 1866 to 1873, as missionary
bishop of Colorado, New Mexico, and Wyoming. He was consecrat-
ed as bishop in January 1866 in Boston's Trinity Episcopal Church

3

before arriving at his new post in Denver. The Boston church name influenced the naming of the new little mission church in Denver. Bishop Spalding was offered a gift of $1,000 from Miss Abby Loring of Boston to build a church as a memorial to Bishop Randall. She specifically requested that the church be named Trinity.

Toward the end of his tenure as missionary bishop, the Rt. Rev. Randall observed the rapid growth of Denver on its eastern edge of town. He envisioned a new Episcopal parish on that growing edge of the city. However, he died September 28, 1873 before realizing his vision.

Following the death of Bishop Randall, his successor, the Rt. Rev. John Franklin Spalding, picked up where the previous bishop left off. Bishop Spalding quickly affirmed the initiative of the one-and-only Episcopal church (St. John's Church in the Wilderness), which had formed a Sunday school within the growing eastern edge of the city in late November 1873. Its purpose was to lay the ground-work for a new mission parish as envisioned by Bishop Randall. The Sunday school was held in a rented building at Twenty-First Street and Arapahoe. Opening attendance was ninety children.

The vestry of St. John's Church in the Wilderness purchased four lots at the corner of Twenty-Sixth Street and Curtis for the construction of the new mission church. It was built with lightning speed and the Sunday school was transferred to the new building when it opened in June of 1874. Two years later, in 1876, Colorado became a state of the Union.

NEW LITTLE PARISH DEVELOPS

For the next half-century, the fledgling mission evolved into a lively parish. It quickly became known for its music. In the 1890s, the parish formed a chapter of the Brotherhood of St. Andrew's, an Episcopal religious order for men. The Brotherhood focused on social services.

Between the founding of the parish in 1874 and 1919, essen-tially a dozen clergy served Trinity Memorial Chapel. Most of them served four years or less—often just one or two years. Exceptions included the Rev. Charles Marshall, who served fifteen years as rector from 1880 to 1895. The Rev. George Holoran served eleven years, from 1907 to 1918.

Two factors contributed to instability. First was the frequent change of clergy. Second was the instability of the church building, which had been built in haste in 1874. The building required constant repair and upkeep. During the fifteen years of the Rev. Marshall's ministry, the building was improved and expanded to seat 350 parishioners in 1883. Shortly after the twentieth century dawned, the parish made the decision to replace the deteriorating structure with a brand-new building.

For five years, parishioners worshipped in various temporary quarters. Eventually, the parish identified its new home within the boundaries of the Cathedral Close on the 2000 block of Glenarm Place. Ralph Adams Cram was chosen as the architect to design and build the church. Widely known in the U.S. and abroad for his Gothic Revival style churches and schools, Mr. Cram's new church was the only building he designed in Colorado. The small house of worship shares similarities with Mr. Cram's own private chapel he built for himself in 1912 in Sudbury, Massachusetts.

In August 1908 the cornerstone was laid for the new church building. On January 17, 1909 Trinity Memorial Church was dedicated at 2015 Glenarm Place.

Instability of clergy tenure was also accompanied by instability of finances in the development of the little church on the edge of downtown. The parish began its life in June 1874 as a mission of the only other Episcopal church in Denver, St. John's Church in the Wilderness. By September 1875, Trinity Memorial *Chapel* gained financial independence and parish status. It was henceforth known as Trinity Memorial *Church*. Additional periods of mission status occurred three more times when the struggling parish required outside financial support: 1919–1925, 1948, and 1986–2000.

Ten years after building its second church edifice, the parish shifted again to mission status for a second time. On November 25, 1918, the Rev. Henry Steele, rector of the parish, met with the bishop and trustees of the Colorado Episcopal Diocese. Their purpose was to develop a strategy to enable the congregation to receive additional funds for meeting parish outreach goals. The outcome was that the little parish was converted to mission status and became a mission of the diocese. By agreeing to change the parish name to St. Andrew's Mission, the parish became eligible for more financial support and was able to focus more effectively on systematic pastoral work in the downtown district. With a new location, new building, and new name, a new direction began to unfold.

SHIFTING LANDSCAPE—SHIFTING VISION

With the new decade of the 1920s, a significant new chapter began at St. Andrew's Mission with the arrival of the Rev. Neil Stanley. By 1925–1926, St. Andrew's regained parish status and was thereafter known as St. Andrew's Episcopal Church. Social service within the Denver community began to emerge as a signature ministry of the little church on the edge of downtown.

In 1948, St. Andrew's Episcopal Church transitioned again to mission status. The little church was envisioned as a unique diocesan mission focused on Denver's urban center. Therefore, the diocese once more assumed financial support for its ministries. Bishop Harold Bowen served as the parish rector and the Rev. Gordon Graser served as vicar.

The diocese was keenly aware of the unique population immediately surrounding St. Andrew's church building. Planted upon the soil of the nineteenth-century Cathedral Close, the parish served a neighborhood of large hotels, downtown businesses, and the financial district.

Neighbors also came from apartment houses and rooming houses. The population assimilated Japanese Americans who were recently released from a World War II internment camp in the southern part of Colorado. Neighbors also included Spanish Americans within a Denver melting pot of nationalities.

At the midpoint in the twentieth century, St. Andrew's life centered on liturgical and educational ministries. In the late 1940s and into the 1950s, the parish offered the following ministries.

Sunday Services	Weekday Services Mon.–Fri.	Saturday Afternoon
8:00 a.m. Eucharist	7:30 a.m. Morning Eucharist	5:00–6:00 p.m. confessions or consultations
9:30 a.m. Children's Eucharist		
11:00 a.m. Eucharist		
8:00 p.m. Evensong		

For children, the activities included Altar Boys, Junior Altar Guild for Girls, Choir Boys, Church School, and Monday afternoon catechism.

SEEING WITH NEW EYES

Like a reflection of Mother Nature, the earthly soil of the Cathedral Close began to bear fruit after a period of gestation. The 2000 block of Glenarm Place first took root as ecclesiastic soil in the latter quarter of the nineteenth century. Within the first quarter of the twentieth century, milestones of social justice work began to appear and continued into the early twenty-first century.

The fruit of the Spirit manifested itself as ministries of healthcare and education for those in need. These particular ministries were the same fruits that were first envisioned by the Rt. Rev. John Franklin Spalding in 1874. Bishop Spalding's initial schools and hospital set an example for what was yet to be.

Starting with the Rev. Neil Stanley's vision (1920–1942) of a children's convalescent home followed by a school, the twentieth century continued to produce healthcare and educational ministries like a Holy Orchard.

The Rev. Jon Marr Stark (1969–1984) envisioned food, shelter, education, and healthcare for young people living on the streets of Denver.

The Rev. Kenneth Near (1986–1991) welcomed outcasts from the gay community during the AIDS crisis.

The Rev. Connie Delzell's ministries (1991–2007) followed through by providing housing for those dying of AIDS. Her ministries also served major educational needs of inner-city children, including the establishment of a second Episcopal school.

The next five chapters in this book detail the adventures of these pioneering ministries. One short chapter reveals the fruits of a drought period when social justice ministries continued as the Holy Orchard appeared next to extinction.

Completing the chapters of each of the twentieth-century social justice ministries are the stories of the full context of parish life. Worship, monastic life, faith development, congregational development, music and arts, and interaction with the diocese complete the picture. Ministries to the common good of Denver were grounded in the nourishing life of the Spirit of God.

PARISH CLERGY 1874–PRESENT

Trinity Memorial Church, 1874–1919

1. Walter Howard Moore (interim), 1874–1875
2. Charles Nelson Allen, 1875–1878
3. John Quick Archdeacon, 1879–1880
4. Henry Harrison Haynes, 1878–1880
5. Charles H. Marshall, 1880–1895
6. Daniel L.V. Moffett, 1896
7. Charles Ysla Grimes, 1897–1901
8. Arthur G.H. Bode, 1901–1904
9. Pelham Williams, 1904–1906
10. George H. Holoran, 1907–1918
11. Henry Steele, 1918–1919

St. Andrew's Episcopal Church, 1919–Present

12. Thomas J. Haldeman, 1919–1920
13. Neil Edmund Stanley, 1920–1942
14. Charles D. Evans, 1942–1948
15. Gordon L. Graser, 1949–1954
16. Justin A. Van Lopik, 1954–1969

17. Jon Marr Stark, 1969–1984
18. Cecil Franklin (interim), 1984–1986
19. Kenneth M. Near, 1986–1991
20. Ernest Priest (interim), 1991
21. Constance K. Delzell, 1991–2007
22. Carol Meredith (interim), 2007–2009
23. Elizabeth Randall, 2009–present

DOCUMENTS CONSULTED

Breck, *Episcopal Church in Colorado: 1860–1963*
"Church Consecration," *Rocky Mountain News*, September 14, 1875
Goodstein et al., *Historic Map*
Journal of the Primary Council of the Protestant Episcopal Church in Colorado (pp. 31–33), November 1918
Trinity Memorial Chapel Parish Register, 1874–1880
"The Mission Church of St. Andrew," *Colorado Episcopalian*, October 1949
White, *Colorado Episcopal Clergy in the Nineteenth Century*

PEOPLE CONSULTED

Ethan Anthony, principal architect, Cram and Ferguson Architects, Concord, Massachusetts
Connie Delzell, rector, St. Andrew's Episcopal Church, 1991–2007
Ken Miller, historical conservationist, Denver, Colorado
Ken Near, vicar, St. Andrew's Episcopal Church, 1986–1991
Merrie Need, historian, St. Anne's Episcopal School, Denver, Colorado
Jon Marr Stark (aka Jon Aidan Marr), rector, St. Andrew's Episcopal Church, 1969–1984

2

The Rev. Neil Edmund Stanley

Rector of St. Andrew's Episcopal Church
1920–1942

I have always prayed for you, where knowledge is imperfect
and prayer is frequently mistaken. So always I shall pray for
you, and shortly, where knowledge is complete and where
prayer is omnipotence of prayer.

—From Fr. Stanley's farewell message
read to the congregation October 25, 1942,
one month before his death, November 30, 1942

The Rev. Neil Edmund Stanley is consistently remembered as the
beloved theologian/historian and spiritual leader of St. Andrew's
Episcopal Church by those who knew him and those who came
after him. Fr. Stanley is the longest-serving rector of the parish. His
ministry stretched over twenty-two years, and his legacy shaped the
parish for years to come.

Earlier periods of parish life focused on establishing the little
parish on the edge of downtown. Other periods dealt with developing

the fledging congregation. Fr. Stanley brought the revitalizing power of the Oxford Movement to the forty-six-year-old church.

Throughout Christian history, the church has attempted to serve as a bridge between the sacred and the secular. In the mid-nineteenth century, the Church of England was tilted heavily toward the worldly. In response, the Oxford Movement emerged to restore the English Church to its Catholic heritage and to "right the balance." The Movement, also known as the Anglo-Catholic Movement or Renewal or Revival, recalled the English Church to its ancient apostolic order and to the catholic (universal) doctrines of the early church. Such an emphasis was called "High Church" because it gave a "high" place to the importance of bishops in governance, to the sacraments, and to liturgical worship.

Anglo-Catholic liturgical and devotional customs borrowed heavily from traditions before the English Reformation as well as contemporary Roman Catholic traditions and called for high standards of worship. High Church reforms restored the centrality of the Eucharist and called for the beautification of churches, the chanting of services and hymns, altar hangings, candles, flowers, and the wearing of vestments.

Closely related to worship was personal and corporate devotions along with pastoral and moral care, especially among the poor and dispossessed.

BIOGRAPHICAL BACKGROUND

Born May 7, 1890 in Lawrence, Kansas, Neil Stanley grew up in Kansas with parents who originated in the Midwest and East Coast. His father, Emery Frederick Stanley (1858–1938), was born in Amo, Indiana. He served as a school principal at the Quincey School, Topeka, Kansas. He eventually became an instructor at the University of Kansas (Lawrence). He came from a Quaker background.

Stanley's mother, Annie Ellsworth Wood Stanley (1862–1958), was born in Maryland and was from a Unitarian background. She married Emery Frederick Stanley in 1889.

First-born Neil (1890) was followed by brother Donald Frank Stanley (1891–1978) and sister Catherine Field Stanley (1893–1992). Catherine married Charles Sturtevant.

Half-brother Wendell A. Stanley (1887–1918) and brother Richard Wood Stanley, who died in infancy, completed the family.

EDUCATION AND INITIAL CAREER

Neil Stanley attended the University of Kansas (Lawrence). He graduated from the Washburn College of Law (Topeka) with an LLB degree in 1912. He was preparing for the Kansas bar examination when an unexplained turn of events occurred.

He entered Seabury Theological Seminary in Faribault, Minnesota in 1913. He completed the BD degree in 1916. Postgraduate work was done later in his career at the University of Kansas and Harvard University.

Stanley was ordained a deacon in the Episcopal Church in 1914 and a priest June 11, 1916 in Lawrence, Kansas.

From 1916 to 1919, Stanley served as a member of the faculty at Seabury Seminary. He taught philosophy, psychology, and logic. His draft registration record for 1917–1918 indicated an exemption for ministry.

In 1919 Stanley served as a curate in East Orange, New Jersey. Toward the end of the year on November 1, 1919, Episcopal Bishop Irving P. Johnson (Colorado) called Stanley to be in charge of the Associate Missions in Denver. The Associates included Emmanuel, Epiphany, and St. Andrew's Episcopal missions. The Associates were tasked with providing the chaplaincy of St. Luke's Hospital and the ministrations of the church in the Church Home for Convalescents, the Denver County Hospital, and the Old Ladies' Home.

On January 4, 1920, Stanley became rector of St. Andrew's Episcopal Mission, the axis of the Associate Mission experiment. By the middle of the decade, St. Andrew's regained parish status and became financially independent.

The Rev. Neil Edmund Stanley

The Rev. Neil Stanley, ca. 1920

DENVER'S HISTORICAL CONTEXT

During Stanley's first six years in Denver, the Ku Klux Klan infiltrated the city and developed significant political power. At the height of their reign (1923–1925), the KKK could boast that their members included 1) the mayor of Denver, Benjamin Stapleton, 2) the governor of Colorado, Clarence Morley, 3) the majority of members in the Colorado House of Representatives, and 4) the Denver City Council.

During this time frame, KKK members penetrated every part of Denver's fabric of life. Members invaded small businesses, college campuses, private social clubs, neighborhood organizations, and media; and, sadly, they infiltrated churches.

The KKK's leader was known as the Grand Dragon. His name was John Galen Locke. His home was just seven blocks down the street from St. Andrew's Episcopal Mission. The church stood in the 2000 block of Glenarm Place and the Grand Dragon resided in the 1300 block.

John Galen Locke was an Episcopalian on paper. He served as the baptismal sponsor of Mayor Benjamin Stapleton's first-born son, who was baptized at St. Mark's Episcopal Church—another downtown Episcopal church in Denver.

Mayor Stapleton's wife, Mabel Freeland Stapleton, was the organist at All Saints Episcopal Church in the Highlands section north of downtown. Seventy-five years later a white Klan robe was discovered while cleaning a storage area of the church. The Highlands was a highly concentrated neighborhood of Klan members in the 1920s.

The KKK's primary targets in Denver were twofold: Catholics and Jews. In a stroke of irony, a 1920 letter by a member of St. Andrew's Episcopal Mission was written to the vestry at the same time that Fr. Stanley began his ministry at the parish on January 4, 1920. The letter was dated January 7, 1920. Stanley was affirmed by the bishop in introducing Anglo-Catholic liturgy and practices to the parish. The parish letter writer strongly objected to Catholic practices. Excerpts from the letter follow.

> To the Wardens and Vestry of St. Andrews Church and those assembled:
>
> I have sung in the choir of this church for the past twenty-eight years and have missed during that period few services or choir rehearsals; also have very seldom raised my voice in complaint or otherwise at meetings of the church.
>
> With the above record to my credit I ask your attention while I relieve my mind of a few things. One of the greatest scourges of the world today is the political machine, known as the Roman Catholic Church. They have in all ages through bloodshed, lies, intrigue, managed to rule and control nations and peoples, always covering their real actions and motives under the cloak of Christianity.

Much of Mr. Raup's letter is a repetition of charges against the Roman Catholic Church. He makes clear his veneration of Low Church practices, with which he is familiar. He ends his letter with a final reiteration of his distaste for Roman Catholic customs.

The ritual and in fact the entire service of this St. Andrew's Church is absolutely beautiful and we are trying to keep it so and are proud of it; why, then, is it necessary that we begin to ape the Roman Church—why is it necessary that a woman of the church who does lots of good and whom we all like, should parade before us the garments of a sister of charity of the Roman political machine ... Why should it be necessary that we wear the many colored vestments that are part of every Roman Mass and why is it necessary to have incense ascending in clouds in order to worship God in the right way. I would be ashamed to be thot [*sic*] a Roman Catholic by anyone, but to belong to a church which is aping the Romans, appears to be far worse.

I am not dictating to those learned gentlemen who are to help us, but consider my years of service to justify your listening to the statement of my steadfast intention to stand by the old service that is dear to me.

Yours respectfully, E.O. Raup [Eli Raup][1]

In the little parish of St. Andrew's Episcopal Mission, Fr. Stanley encountered some inevitable internal pushback as evidenced by Mr. Raup's letter, as well as the external strident voices of the KKK, which spread hatred against Catholics and Jews in both word and deed throughout the city of Denver.

STANLEY'S ANGLO-CATHOLIC LEGACIES IN WORSHIP

In 1920, it was common practice throughout the Colorado Episcopal diocese for urban parishes to worship according to Low Church traditions. A notable exception was the Episcopal Church of the Redeemer, Denver, which began Anglo-Catholic worship in 1893.

1. Raup, letter to St. Andrew's vestry, January 7, 1920.

The Rev. Neil Stanley in his Anglo-Catholic vestments, ca. 1930

Innovative practices included those mentioned in E. O. Raup's letter. Changes such as colorful vestments worn by the clergy, in contrast to the simple black cassock and white surplice of Low Church worship, and the introduction of incense would have been instituted by Stanley. Eli Raup also referred in his letter to the wooden confessional booth in the back of the nave and the nun's habit worn by the Episcopal nun, Sister Adah Gabriel. Sister Adah was a member of the Episcopal religious order known as the Sisters of St. John the Evangelist and assigned to the St. Andrew's parish in 1919.

Beyond Mr. Raup's naming of Anglo-Catholic practices, it is unknown how extensively Fr. Stanley changed the specifics of the liturgy. Although Stanley began the process of change, it took a period of years for full development of the Anglo-Catholic liturgy within the wider Episcopal Church. The 1979 *Book of Common Prayer* was the culmination of that process.

The processional we see today is led by the verger carrying the ancient symbol of a verge (medieval protective weapon). He is followed by the acolyte carrying the cross. In addition, the processional includes the carrying of lit candles, which are then placed in stands next to the altar during worship. Another part of the procession involves carrying the Bible held high and then placing it on the altar. In addition, the thurifer carries the thurible of incense in procession—swinging it from side to side. Accompanying the thurifer may be the boat boy—a very young parishioner who carries a supply of incense to replenish the thurible.

As the processional reaches the chancel, the clergy cense the altar with the thurible.

A current-day practice at St. Andrew's that presumably originated with Fr. Stanley is the custom of rector and deacon genuflecting (kneeling with one knee) in front of the tabernacle, containing the reserved elements of the Eucharist, before proceeding to their respective chairs.

Today's reading of the Gospel lesson involves the deacon moving from the chancel, carrying the Bible high above his/her head, led by a verger and accompanied by acolytes with tall processional candles. The small procession proceeds from altar to midway in the center aisle, where the deacon censes the Bible before reading the Gospel scripture of the day. Whether this custom was initiated by Stanley is unknown.

Gestures by parishioners during this changing time would likely have included the right hand making the sign of the cross at key points during the liturgy. In addition, the gesture of genuflecting (kneeling with one knee) before entering the pew was another likely change. Facing and bowing to the cross as it moved in procession and was in alignment with each person was another, as was bowing whenever moving in front of the altar.

Prominent within Anglo-Catholic worship is the centrality of the Eucharist. In Low Church practice, the Eucharist was typically celebrated once a month. Sunday services consisted of Morning Prayer. In Anglo-Catholic churches, the Eucharist is typically celebrated daily and often several times on Sunday. From Stanley's era onward, St. Andrew's frequently included daily and Sunday celebrations of the Eucharist. In addition, the term "Mass" was commonly used to refer to the Eucharist. The ringing of a bell at key points in the Eucharist/Mass is another Anglo-Catholic practice. Additional elements include the washing of hands by clergy at the beginning of the Communion service, raising up high the sacrament during its consecration, and the consuming of leftover crumbs and wine at the end of the service. The ambry lamp hangs over the tabernacle, holding the reserved sacrament, which is taken by the priest to those who are ill.

Further Anglo-Catholic traditions include altar frontals (cloths). Clothing of the clergy typically included birettas (three-cornered hats). Parish photos depict Stanley's successors wearing birettas into the 1950s. Anglo-Catholic clergy of the mid-twentieth century often wore their liturgical cassocks (long-sleeved, floor-length garments) along with a clerical collar at *all* times—not just during church services.

The Stations of the Cross reflect Anglo-Catholic influence. Fr. Stanley introduced devotional booklets by the Episcopal Order of the Holy Cross (West Park, New York) that were used for the Stations of the Cross.

Artistic work reflected the Anglo-Catholic emphasis on devotion to Mary. During Stanley's tenure, religious artist Marion Buchan made the *Gothic Virgin* sculpture and the *Byzantine Madonna* sculpture. Today these iconic figures remain. The *Byzantine Madonna* stands to the right of the lectern in the nave. The *Gothic Virgin* is the centerpiece of the side chapel to the left of the chancel.

The veneration of saints has a prominent place in Anglo-Catholic culture, particularly patron saints such as St. Andrew in this parish. The wooden sculpture of St. Andrew, which now stands in the side chapel to the right of the chancel, was donated in the 1960s by Verna Schneider.

Such veneration of saints also included praying to the saints. Primary among the saints is Mary, the mother of Jesus. Sometimes the Hail Mary prayer was used along with the rosary. Among Fr. Stanley's closest colleagues at St. Andrew's was Sister Adah Gabriel, who worked with him from 1919 until her death in 1933. At the time of her death, Stanley said, "I don't know whether to pray *for* her or *to* her."[2]

Anglo-Catholic music in the U.S. developed largely through the Rev. Charles Winfred Douglas. Fr. Douglas was the primary musician of the wider Episcopal Church—somewhat like its musician-in-chief during the first half of the twentieth century. He composed or arranged music for the emerging Anglo-Catholic worship services. Singing the liturgy became more the norm. Examples of his arrangements are found in the current Episcopal hymnal.

Fr. Douglas served as a canon (clergy staff) at St. John's Episcopal Cathedral in Denver at the same time that Fr. Stanley served at St. Andrew's. The two clergymen collaborated together on a book of prayers for every occasion called *A Manual for Priests of the American Church—A Supplement to the Book of Common Prayer*. It was published posthumously (1944) shortly after both men died. It was republished in 2004 by Wipf and Stock Publishers.

Anglo-Catholic tradition includes the presence of holy water, usually near the entrance of the church. Today a wooden wall plaque with holy water is dedicated "in loving memory of Rev. Neil Stanley" at the back of the nave. Anglo-Catholic practice includes dipping one's fingers in the holy water upon entering the church and then crossing oneself with the right hand when entering the holy space of the nave. The custom reflects a spiritual preparation for entering holy space. It reminds parishioners of their baptismal vows and symbolizes the letting go of worldly cares in order to enter the sanctuary with open hearts and minds.

2. Stanley, sermon, January 15, 1933, 2.

Holy water font located in St. Andrew's Episcopal Church nave

On a lighter note, terms of address changed with the advent of Anglo-Catholic practices. During the preceding Low Church era, clergy were addressed as "Mister" and considered to be "ministers." That changed with Anglo-Catholic customs. Clergy now were addressed as "Reverend" or "Father" and were considered to be "priests" of the church.

STANLEY'S LEGACY MOVES BEYOND THE PARISH

Anglo-Catholic worship was the hallmark of the Oxford Movement of the nineteenth century. However, as Stanley exemplified, the Movement also emphasized pastoral and moral care beyond the church doors.

We learn about his pastoral care through his meticulous record keeping. The parish register from 1925 to 1932 is full of details entered in Fr. Stanley's own hand.

He recorded an astonishing number of baptisms for orphans from the Denver Orphan Train. Over one thousand such baptisms were carried out by Stanley in the period between 1925 and 1932.

The Denver Orphan Train was part of a national supervised welfare program that transported orphans and homeless and abandoned children from large Eastern cities to other regions of the United States from 1853 to 1930. The primary cities "exporting" children were Boston, Philadelphia, and New York City. A major organizer of the Orphan Train Movement was the Children's Aid Society of the New York Foundling Hospital. Other organizing agencies also developed.

The Children's Aid Society worked with various organizations to prearrange for placement of the children. A strong demand for children came from farmers and ranchers who could not have children of their own but needed workers on their land. However, urban families also served as foster homes. Local screening committees provided on-site processing.

Denver General Hospital apparently served as a processing center. Sister Adah Gabriel from St. Andrew's was a social worker. She appears to have been a critical link between Denver General Hospital and St. Andrew's. Most of the baptisms took place at the hospital. Sister Adah served as baptismal sponsor of nearly all the baptisms, with Fr. Stanley serving as the officiate. After the Sisters of St. Anne established a chapter in Denver in 1929, Mother Superior Noel also assisted in the orphan baptisms. A few of the baptisms took place at the properties of the Sisters of St. Anne.

Careful reading of the parish register reveals the date, name, age, place of baptism, sponsor, officiate, and occasionally notation of the death of the orphan. It reads like a storybook of a poignant chapter in our national and local history.

During its existence, the Orphan Train Movement relocated about two hundred thousand children. The program ended with the beginning of organized foster care in the U.S. around 1930. The Orphan Train Heritage Society of America is headquartered in Springdale, Arkansas. The National Orphan Train Museum and Research Center is in Concordia, Kansas.

Fr. Stanley's and Sister Adah's participation with the Denver Orphan Train reflects the commitment to both sacramental and pastoral care components of the Oxford Movement. It also reflects the inclusive and outgoing nature of pastoral and moral care as understood by the proponents of the Movement.

MONASTIC REVIVALS OF THE OXFORD MOVEMENT

Fr. Stanley's legacy engaged various strands of the Oxford Movement, one of which was Episcopal religious orders. During the Oxford Movement, a revival of monastic life occurred within the Anglican churches in England and Episcopal churches in the U.S. The very first religious community for men in the Anglican Church since the Reformation was the Society of St. John the Evangelist, founded in 1866 in England. Four years later, in 1870, Richard Meux Benson established a chapter in Boston, where the U.S. religious order has been headquartered ever since in next-door Cambridge.

Sister Adah Gabriel was originally a member of the Sisterhood of St. John the Evangelist. The Denver chapter was founded in 1904 by Colorado Bishop Charles Olmsted. The chapter was dissolved in 1920 by Colorado Bishop Irving Peake Johnson when the group diminished to the last one or two nuns.

Sister Adah later became a nun with the Sisters of St. Anne at the end of her life. In fact, Mother Noel inducted her into the order just hours before Sister Adah died. This may have been so that the St. Anne Sisters could provide a proper burial for the nun, who had been such a good friend of the order.

Sister Adah Gabriel was born in England in 1862 and died in Denver in 1933. During her seventy years, she not only served as a nun, she was also a social worker. From 1919 to 1933, she was assigned by the bishop to serve within St. Andrew's parish. Sister Adah and Fr. Stanley worked closely together.

Fr. Stanley's sermon at her funeral on January 15, 1933 paints a picture of her devoted life of service. He spoke of "her fearlessness, her faithfulness, and her selflessness."[3] He indicated she did not know the meaning of fear. Stanley spoke of "the ugly and repellent side of life" she encountered daily as a social worker. She talked about the people among whom she worked as "beautiful souls."

Stanley also remembered her as "the most utterly selfless person I have ever known." He further described her: "She could, on occasion, be as ruthless, as inflexible, as a cataclysm of nature. But there was always something engaging, something disarming, about her sheer selflessness that few ever found the heart to resist."

"To think of life's common landscape without her gives one a sort of vertigo," recounted Fr. Stanley as he mourned her steadying presence. "It is as if one were to look at the mountains only to find Pike's Peak no longer there."

His closing remarks spoke of her as a saint among the Saints: "Among the Holy Souls, she does pray for us."[4]

Sister Adah was buried in the small burial grounds at St. Anne's in the Hills retreat center near Morrison, Colorado. Her grave marker is the only one that differs from all the other small, flat markers next to the ground: it is marked by a tall tombstone as if to signal to the world that she stands out among her peers in perpetuity.

Following her death, the parish paid tribute to Sister Adah by forming the Sister Adah Guild. It was the hospitality committee that served meals for parish events. The Guild was active for many years.

THE SISTERS OF ST. ANNE

Again, we see the result of the Oxford Movement giving birth to a resurgence of religious orders both in England and the United States. The seminal order— the Society of St. John the Evangelist— was the first to emerge in the city of Oxford, England (1866). Then in 1870 it expanded to the United States, settling in the neighborhood

3. Stanley, sermon, 2.
4. Stanley, sermon, 2.

of Harvard University in Cambridge, Massachusetts. In England, the men's order (the Society of St. John the Evangelist) sponsored a women's order, which was named after St. Anne, the mother of Mary, who gave birth to Jesus. It almost seems like a reflection of apostolic succession—with inclusion of both men and women.

In 1910, the Order of St. Anne was organized in the Boston area of Arlington Heights, Massachusetts. The two founders were Ethelred Barry and the Rev. Frederick Cecil Powell. Fr. Powell served as the superior of the Society of St. John the Evangelist, Cambridge. Mother Ethelred was the first superior of the Order of St. Anne in Arlington Heights.

PARTNERSHIP OF PARISH AND SISTERS

In the late 1920s, physicians within the parish of St. Andrew's Episcopal Church prompted the rector, Fr. Neil Stanley, to take action to establish a convalescent home for children with chronic illnesses in Denver because there was none. Fr. Stanley contacted the Sisters of St. Anne in Arlington Heights and asked for a contingent to be sent to Denver for that purpose. Stanley's long ministry was enhanced and extended by his partnership with the Sisters of St. Anne, a religious order primarily of nurses and teachers. Together the priest and sisters lived out the pastoral and moral care component of the Oxford Movement.

In April 1929, a contingent of three sisters arrived in Denver to establish a chapter of their order and to found their convalescent home for children with chronic illnesses such as rheumatic fever, typhoid, and tuberculosis. By the 1940s, polio was the centerpiece of their work. Their superior was Mother Noel Juanita, originally from England, a nurse who gained experience in World War I. She became a nun in the Order of St. Anne in England following the World War. Later she moved to the Boston area, where she was part of the Sisters of St. Anne in Arlington Heights. The mandate of the order was to pray and to care for children.

Mother Noel (1888–1971) was the founding mother superior of the Sisters of St. Anne chapter in Denver, 1929.

St. Andrew's Episcopal Church leased Twin Houses across the street from the parish at 2050 and 2054 Glenarm Place for the purposes of housing the convent and the convalescent home.

Twin Houses at 2050 and 2054 Glenarm Place served as the original location of St. Anne's Convalescent Home and Convent in Denver in 1929.

Women of the parish held a linen shower to provide sheets and towels for the sisters' new home. One of the parishioners, Mrs. William West Grant II (Gertrude Hendrie Grant), provided furnishings for the sisters' convent and convalescent home.

Fr. Stanley became the chaplain for the sisters and was named warden in charge of business and property for the order. He continued in this dual role until his death in 1942. Parishioner William West Grant II served as attorney for the sisters until his death in 1957. Fr. Stanley and Mr. Grant also bought several lots immediately adjacent to the church on the north to hold in trust for the Sisters of St. Anne, anticipating that they might establish their convent there.

Shortly after the sisters arrived in Denver, Fr. Stanley shared his dual vision for their ministry in the city. His immediate goal was for them to establish a convalescent home for children with chronic illnesses, which they did within days after arriving. Stanley's long-term goal was for the sisters to establish a coeducational school for girls and boys. The sisters accomplished both. As their journey unfolded, they focused on the convalescent home for twenty years. When new medical treatments and vaccines developed, they shifted focus and established a school.

The sisters were warmly welcomed within the diocese as well as by the St. Andrew's parishioners. Four months after arriving, they were invited by the Rev. Charles Winfred Douglas to vacation in Evergreen, Colorado in one of his Evergreen Conference Center buildings.

Within the parish, the sisters taught Sunday school, led women's retreats, engaged in parish visitations, worked with the acolytes, and led summer camps for children.

Parishioner Gertrude Hendrie Grant was an influential member of the congregation who was also a member of the Junior League. In 1931, the Junior League offered their farm property at 2701 South York Street to the sisters for their convalescent home. The sisters then relocated to the South York estate, which they developed into a large and accommodating facility.

In the same year, the Episcopal Church of the Ascension in Denver also gave mountain property of seventeen acres near Morrison, Colorado to the sisters. It became known as St. Anne's in the

Hills and was used as a retreat and educational center by the sisters. It had both an outdoor chapel and indoor chapel along with dormitories for visiting children and a small burial grounds. Sister Adah, who became a sister of St. Anne on her deathbed, was the first sister to be buried at St. Anne's in the Hills.

In the twenty-first century, a former summer camper at St. Anne's in the Hills, Gertie Grant (granddaughter of Gertrude Grant), remembers with humor the morning inspection of their dormitories at the retreat center. One of the sisters taught Gertie to use a wire coat hanger to smooth the covers of her bed to assure the passing of inspection. Gertie also took joy in the creative crafts of the summer camp.[5]

GROWTH AND EXPANSION OF SISTERS OF ST. ANNE'S WORK

Not only did the order expand and grow, from three sisters to over a dozen, so too did their substantial and effective nursing care.

1929

St. Anne's Home was the only convalescent home for children in the state of Colorado. From the beginning, Mother Noel incorporated two medical doctors from Denver Children's Hospital to assist in the work of St. Anne's Home. "Young patients were too well to be in Children's Hospital yet too frail to go home."[6] The compassionate love of children by the sisters did not stop with a convalescent home. 1) The sisters provided temporary foster care of babies who had been given up for adoption in the first year of their lives. 2) They provided temporary care for youngsters who were severely undernourished and were identified by the Denver Public Schools. 3) Long-term care for a severely mentally impaired child was also provided. 4) Their very first patient was an infant with birth defects that were not capable of repair. He died shortly after the sisters took

5. Gerti Grant, interview, June 17, 2015.
6. Need, "Sisters of St. Anne," 17.

him in. Mother Noel sculpted his image in clay as a way of dealing with her grief. The sculpture became the baby Jesus for the nativity scene at the St. Anne's convent chapel.

1931

The sisters moved from their initial quarters at 2050 and 2054 Glenarm Place to the farm property owned by the Junior League. The League had been operating a preventorium at 2701 South York Street. Its twenty residents were impoverished children who had been exposed to tuberculosis. Their typical stay was three months, to immerse them in fresh air and rest and to prevent their exposure from developing into TB. The sisters took over the property when the preventorium was closed and used it for convalescent care. They also expanded the existing buildings to accommodate their widening services.

Farmhouse and grounds at 2701 South York became the permanent location of St. Anne's Convalescent Home and Convent in 1931.

The Rev. Neil Edmund Stanley

1932–1933

Typical of the sisters' work was ongoing care of orphans. David Lyons was orphaned and sick with rheumatic fever. Mother Noel became his guardian and raised him in the St. Anne convent.[7] During his college years, he lived in the clergy house with Fr. Stanley. David was active in the St. Andrew parish, where he met his future wife. Following World War II, David served as an acolyte trainer of Japanese American and Hispanic American boys from the neighborhood. David and his wife Marge "hung out" with the boys informally, offering them a family-type support group.

1934

Episcopal Bishop Irving Peake Johnson asked Mother Noel to manage the nursing staff at the Oakes Home at 2825 West Thirty-Second Street in north Denver. It was a convalescent facility for adult TB patients and the elderly. The Oakes Home was also in financial distress.

Four of the life-professed nuns moved into the Oakes Home. The novices remained at St. Anne's Home on South York Street. Sister Cecile, who moved to Denver from Boston with Mother Noel, served as the novice mistress at the York Street facility. The two locations offered consistently high-quality care for their patients. By 1935, the Oakes Home had doubled its patients from twenty to forty and was debt free.

In February 1936, a bitterly cold winter briefly closed St. Anne's Home because of insufficient heating. The South York Street children were temporarily transferred to the Oakes Home and into an empty house originally designed to house nurses. As winter warmed up, infants and girls remained at the Oakes facility while kindergarteners and older boys returned to St. Anne's Home.

7. Lyons, letter to Rev. Delzell, September 14, 2005.

1937

Considerable construction and expansion of facilities took place in 1936–1937 at St. Anne's Home. As a result, all the children returned to St. Anne's Home on South York. Its new capacity could shelter fifty children.

1941

The Sisters of St. Anne ended their work at the Oakes Home and returned to their campus at 2701 South York. This brought back together the life-professed sisters and the novices: a total of thirteen nuns. Meanwhile, the diocese eventually sold the Oakes estate to the Order of the Poor of Sisters of St. Francis.

1942

The polio epidemic, which began in 1935, was at its height. In the long story of Denver's battle with polio treatment, the Sisters of St. Anne played a significant role. Denver, the only city in the state with polio treatment options, had an acute shortage of nurses and facilities. Polio cases in Colorado numbered nearly one thousand.

During the 1940s, St. Anne's Convalescent Home specialized in treatment of polio for children from throughout Colorado.

Rural families in Colorado were especially hard hit. They needed all family members to work on the farms and ranches. In addition, they could not afford special medical needs of polio patients. As a result, some rural parents surrendered their children to the state of Colorado for care. The Sisters of St. Anne became the official and permanent foster parents for one such child, named Nancy Olson.

St. Anne's Home quickly made use of the groundbreaking treatment approach of Sister Kenny of Australia. Sister Kenny moved in 1940 to the U.S., where her successful method for treating polio was enthusiastically adopted by the Mayo Clinic in Rochester, Minnesota as well as by the Sisters of St. Anne in Denver.

"They [sisters] worked six-hour shifts applying the hot cloth. First, they boiled a strip of wool, ran it through a wringer three times, and laid it on the child's skin, wrapping it over the spastic muscles. Next, they applied a layer of oiled silk, which sealed in the moisture. Finally, they laid strips of dry wool on top of the silk to seal the heat within. They did this six times a day for each patient."[8]

Alternating with application of hot packs were massage and exercise. Three Red Cross nurses worked with the thirteen sisters.

St. Anne's Home provided polio care at no cost to the parents. Generous gifts enabled the sisters to purchase special equipment required for the Sister Kenny treatment. The National Foundation for Infantile Paralysis (March of Dimes) contributed to the sisters' work. Ongoing gifts, both large and small, funded the effective polio treatment by the sisters.

Denver's young polio patients began their journey at Children's Hospital. They began by spending two weeks in isolation. No family member or friends were allowed to visit them. During this time, each child was suffering from high fever, pain from muscle spasms, and the fear of dying.

Consequently, when the children entered convalescent care at St. Anne's Home, they brought with them their trauma of forced separation from families. The sisters responded with their signature loving attention. "They administered a grueling protocol of

8. Need, "Sisters of St. Anne," 20.

hot-pack care and massage. They followed up with medical appointments and occupational therapy routines for each patient. They changed the children's clothing and bedding, did the laundry, bathed the children, woke them up and put them to bed, cooked for them, and fed them. They helped them keep up with the schoolwork that their own schools sent them. They also supervised their play, created gardens and playgrounds and special events for them, and kept dogs for the sake of healing the whole child."[9] Clearly, their patient population was limited in order to give this kind of intensive and personalized care.

Mother Noel summed up the experience many years later. Reflecting on the years of the polio epidemic in Denver, she said, "There were eighty polio-stricken children who were carried into St. Anne's. All but one walked out."[10]

1950

By the 1950s, polio and other chronic illnesses began to wane because of vaccines and advances in healthcare. Mother Noel began forming a new purpose for the sisters: a coeducational school for girls and boys, as envisioned by Fr. Stanley in 1929. A new sister who joined the order was Sister Irene. With long experience in teaching, she spearheaded the organization of the Episcopal School of St. Anne and served as mother superior throughout the formative decades of the school. The transformation was a natural one as the ward-size rooms became classrooms.

9. Need, "Sisters of St. Anne," 23.
10. Need, "Sisters of St. Anne," 23.

The Rev. Neil Edmund Stanley

Mother Irene (1900–1996) served as mother superior of the School of St. Anne during 1950s–1990s. She was the last of the Sisters of St. Anne in the Denver chapter.

ONE DOOR CLOSES—ANOTHER OPENS

The Episcopal School of St. Anne was founded in 1950 at 2701 South York Street, just several blocks from the University of Denver. The first year included kindergarten and first grade. More grades were gradually added until 1967, when the school became incorporated. By 1978, the middle school program became fully established. Like the convalescent home, the school campus has gradually added new buildings to accommodate the growing student body. Today the school includes preschool through eighth grade. It offers tuition assistance to some 20 percent of its four-hundred-plus students.

The present-day School of St. Anne administration building is housed in the
original farmhouse given to the Sisters of St. Anne in 1931.

During the twenty-some years of the St. Anne Home, Mother
Noel led the sisters through exceptionally challenging times, beginning with the Great Depression and throughout World War II. As
a woman leader of the first half of the twentieth century, she pio-
neered leadership in development of a religious order, nursing care,
nonstop fundraising, perpetual building expansion, and landscaping a sizeable number of acres. Today the St. Anne's campus boasts
unusual species of trees and plants, along with gardens originally
planted by Mother Noel and sisters following her. Mother Irene
specialized in developing countless varieties of roses.

Listed below is a sampling of some Sisters of St. Anne during
the 1930s–1940s.

Mother Superior Noel Juanita

Sister Adah Gabriel

Sister Cecile

Sister Ellen

Sister Esther

Sister Eunice Mary

Sister Kristen Juanita

Sister Patience

Sister Isabel

Sister Irene

Sister Delphine Schmidt (tertiary member)—parishioner of St. Andrew's Church.

Sister Benigne (tertiary member)—formerly June Benedict, divorced wife of architect Jacques Benedict, designer/builder of the 1928 St Andrew's clergy house. Sister Benigne was also a major benefactress of the order.

Seven of the sisters are buried at St. Anne's in the Hills near Morrison, Colorado. The ashes of the rest are interred in the burial mound on the school grounds at 2701 South York Street, Denver. The last of the sisters from the Denver chapter, Sister Irene, died in 1996.

LEADING LIGHTS OF LEADERSHIP

Two prominent parishioners during Stanley's era were Will and Gertrude Grant. Their formal names were William West Grant II (1881–1957) and Gertrude Hendrie Grant (1886–1956.) They both played key roles in the ministries of the Sisters of St. Anne and other matters of congregational life.

Gertrude Hendrie Grant, an avid birder, is shown with a Cooper's hawk.

35

Originally they were part of the congregation at St. John's Episcopal Cathedral in Denver. One day as Gertrude Grant was visiting with Bishop Irving Peake Johnson, she questioned him about wide-ranging theological and liturgical issues. "Bishop Johnson finally said to her that there was a young priest who could answer all her questions; that he had just come out from Seabury Seminary where he had been a professor; that his name was Neil Stanley, and to go and see him.

"She went. She found him to be a rather shy young man about thirty-four years old, with really a profound knowledge of many things, including human nature and theology; a devastating sense of humor, and quite able to answer anything she could propound."[11]

This was in the early 1920s, shortly after Fr. Stanley became rector of St. Andrew's. The Grants quickly became eager members of St. Andrew's Episcopal parish and continued for three decades until the end of their lives in the mid-1950s.

William West Grant II (Will) with his new grandson, William West Grant IV (Peter), in the early 1930s

11. Grant, *Such Is Life*, 170.

Both Neil Stanley and Will Grant had law school degrees. Although Stanley pursued the ministry, Grant pursued the practice of law in Denver. He also ran (unsuccessfully) as a Democratic candidate for mayor in 1935.

Within the parish, Grant served in a variety of positions. In October 1942 both Grant and his son were elected members of the vestry, with the senior Grant serving as senior warden and his oldest son, Edwin Hendrie Grant (Ned), serving as a vestryman. His longtime work with the Sisters of St. Anne has been previously mentioned.

In his 1952 memoirs, Grant acknowledged some of his primary positions within the Episcopal Church: "... vestryman, junior and senior warden, Diocesan Board of Trustees, Chancellor of the diocese, delegate to General Convention (multiple times), chairman of one of the standing committees of General Convention, member of the National Council of Churches, and numerous committees of the church."[12]

One of the Grant family's distinctive chapters involved Richthofen Castle, where they lived for almost thirty years, from 1910 to 1937. At the time, the castle was on the outskirts of Denver in the Montclair area and bounded by Eleventh Street, Onieda Street, Twelfth Street, and Pontiac Streets. It still stands and is occupied by different owners.

During the Grant family time, three generations of family lived together within the castle's thirty-eight rooms. The patriarch and matriarch were Edwin Beard Hendrie and wife Marion Carnes Hendre. Their only child, Gertrude Hendrie, and her husband, William West Grant II, were the middle generation. And the youngest generation consisted of the three Grant children: Edwin Hendrie Grant (Ned), William West Grant III (Bill), and Melanie Grant.

Middle child Bill Grant wrote about the experiences of growing up in the castle. At the time of the Hendrie-Grant family residence, it was known as Castlewood. He describes the adventure of being sent to a private Episcopal boarding school called St. Stephen's in Colorado Springs. Bill Grant was eight years old and his brother

12. Grant, *Such Is Life*, 178.

Ned was ten years old. "For the first time, we saw in some detail the differences between the sheltered luxury at Castlewood and the way some of the rest of the world lived."[13]

The Hendrie-Grant family pictured at Castlewood in 1928

Bill Grant wrote extensively about the extraordinary lives of the Castlewood clan. He concluded that it was "a scale of luxurious comfort unknown in Denver today. My standard of living has been declining ever since."[14]

A memorable trait of the Grant family was their exuberant enjoyment of fun. The Arapahoe Hunt Club was an example. A retired Episcopal priest within the St. Andrew's parish, the Rev. Richard Palmer, remembers the generation of Bill Grant and his family. It was customary for Bill Grant and his wife, Helen Prindle Grant (known as Pru), to worship as a family with their four children at the 8:00 Morning Prayer service at St. Andrew's in the 1950s. At the stroke of 9:00 a.m. they piled into their family car for the drive

13. Grant, "Castlewood," 5.
14. Grant, "Castlewood," 3.

to the Arapahoe Hunt Club on the southern edge of Denver, which is now known as Highlands Ranch. Their riding excursion began promptly at 10:00 a.m.

When Helen (Pru) Grant died in 2012 with her funeral at St. Andrew's, it ended almost ninety years of three generations of the Grant family at St. Andrew's.

PEOPLE OF THE PARISH

Like all parishes, a diversity of people has participated in the life and ministries of the church. One of the stalwarts during Fr. Neil Stanley's ministry was Delphine Schmidt.

Delphine Schmitt (1893–1959) served as organist and conservator of Fr. Stanley's sermons during his ministry. She is pictured with the Rev. Charles Evans, who succeeded Fr. Stanley in 1942, along with choir boys and acolytes.

Delphine was a single woman of multiple talents. She served as organist during Stanley's ministry. As an accomplished church musician, she regularly participated in the Evergreen (Colorado) Music Conference each summer, where she became friends with conference founder and director Charles Winfred Douglas and his wife, Josephine.

She also served as the archivist of Stanley's sermons. Besides recording them in shorthand, she typed them up, mimeographed many of them, and preserved them. Some were softbound; others were hardbound. A few were published by Gertrude Hendrie Grant in small booklets on a particular theme.

Delphine had undergraduate and graduate degrees in English literature and was particularly fond of both reading and writing poetry. Fr. Stanley was also steeped in literature and poetry, which they shared reciprocally. Delphine's 1934 master's thesis was dedicated to Fr. Stanley with the words, "With many thanks for the guidance without which this never could have been written."[15]

During his last three months of life, Fr. Stanley was hospitalized with cancer of the hip. Among his accomplishments from his hospital bed, he produced a collection of poems, entitled *The Pleasance of Exile*. Two months before his death, he gave the collection to Delphine Schmitt on September 13, 1942. She typed them and preserved them in notebook form.

On May 14, 1931, Delphine became a third-order secular member of the Sisters of St. Anne and was known as Sister Delphine. She served in an auxiliary role, doing work within the convent.

For a period of years, Delphine provided Christmas cards from the British Museum for sale at St. Andrew's. Eventually she organized a scrapbook with samples of these postcard-type cards.

Thanks to Delphine's saving habits, the St. Andrew's archives now hold the Stanley sermon collection, Stanley's last collection of poems, Delphine's master's thesis, and her scrapbook of British Christmas cards.

Outside the church, Delphine worked as advertising manager for Safeway Stores in Denver and later as a customer consultant. Within the Episcopal diocese, she served as editor of the *Colorado Episcopalian* from roughly 1943 to 1949. She was also a correspondent for *The Living Church*, a national Episcopal publication.

Delphine died of cancer on March 26, 1959, at age sixty-five. Following her funeral at St. Andrew's Episcopal Church, she was buried in Colorado Springs, where she grew up.

15. Schmitt, "Tradition of Platonic Mysticism," 1.

A TASTE OF THE NEIGHBORHOOD

During Fr. Stanley's ministry at St. Andrew's, the Titus family came to the parish in the early 1920s. They lived in the neighborhood and were drawn to the Anglo-Catholic services. The family consisted of father Edwin A. Titus (1885–1961) and mother Winifred C. Titus (1887–1963). The couple had three sons. Their oldest was Roderick A. Titus (1912–1996), then John David Titus (1921–1978), followed by Tom Neil Titus (1924–2006).

The parents became quite fond of Fr. Stanley and named their third son after Stanley, giving Tom the middle name of Neil. The Titus family enjoyed recounting the story of young Tom's baptism by Fr. Stanley in 1924. Brother John (age three) shouted out at Fr. Stanley, "Don't bust him, Father!"[16] During baptism, the officiating priest uses a small vessel such as little pitcher or cup to gently pour water over the head of the baby being baptized. In the eyes of a three-year-old, the movement of a small vessel toward the baby's head may seem threatening, hence the shout-out.

The three brothers all became acolytes. By 1927, Roderick was fifteen, John was six, and Tom was three. In that year Roderick served as thurifer, swinging the incense carrier in procession. Six-year-old John served as the boat boy, carrying the supply of incense in procession. And three-year-old Tom was the youngest acolyte— but already in training to become a boat boy like big brother John.

The acolytes in the 1920s wore clothing identical to the children's choir. Their long cassocks were red with white surplices (short, loose-fitting gowns with wide sleeves) and red capes. They also had white ruffled collars and red caps.

16. "Tribute to Tom Titus."

Young Titus brothers, John, age five (left) and Tom, age two, are shown with Emmett Jones, who is mentoring the young boat boys, ca. 1926.

Fr. Stanley routinely served breakfast to his eight acolytes on Sunday mornings. It was a popular custom.

Members of the Titus family continued from the 1920s into the twenty-first century at St. Andrew's. In 1942, Edwin Titus (the father of the family) was elected junior warden of the vestry. Tragically, in 1978 John Titus fell on the ice at age fifty-seven and fractured his skull. His funeral was held at St. Andrew's and his ashes were inurned within the altar. The parish columbarium contains the ashes of all three Titus brothers: John, who died in 1978, followed by Roderick, who died in 1996, and Tom, who died in 2006.

BUILDING OF THE CLERGY HOUSE

Early in Rev. Stanley's ministry, a clergy house was envisioned for the church property. By the mid-1920s, Jacques Benedict was commissioned to design and build a home for the clergyman at

2013 Glenarm Place, next door to the 1908 church building. Ralph Adams Cram was the architect and builder of the 1908 structure. Denver's prominent Gothic Revival architect, Jacques Benedict, carefully crafted the St. Andrew's clergy house to match the original Cram design for church and rectory.

Completed in 1928, the clergy house was designed by Jacques Benedict. An archway connects the clergy house and church building, which was built in 1908.

Prior to the construction of the clergy house, Fr. Stanley originally lived at 1020 West Twelfth Avenue and later at 1956 Grant Avenue—two blocks from the St. Andrew's parish. The Grant Avenue home was a boarding house typical of the era.

By 1928, Fr. Stanley was established in his expansive new residence side by side with the church. Its roominess complemented Stanley's natural hospitality. It quickly became a welcoming place for parish visitors, those needing comfort and haven, neighborhood boys for morning breakfasts, and a center of parish life. To keep the household running smoothly, Fr. Stanley hired a housekeeper.

The clergy house served as a home for St. Andrew's rectors for nearly sixty years. By the late 1980s the building was renovated and became known as the Parish House for church offices and parish activities.

ASSISTANTS SERVING WITH FR. STANLEY

During the twenty-two years that Fr. Stanley served as rector, a variety of officiates assisted him. In the parish register of 1925–1932, Fr. Stanley listed a dozen assistants who came and went over the years.

Among those whose names appeared most frequently in the parish register of baptisms and official ministrations—in the absence of Fr. Stanley—were Tom J. Halderman, J. W. Hudston, William L. Hogg, Willis D. Nutting, and Ralph J. Rohr.

During summers, Fr. Stanley often spent several months in England. Therefore, it was during the summer months that his assistants took over the clerical tasks. During the 1920s, when the Denver Orphan Train was active, baptisms were extraordinarily frequent. The parish register indicates that both Sister Adah Gabriel and Mother Superior Noel of the Sisters of St. Anne also served "in extremis" for baptisms in the absence of rector or assistant.

One of the longest-serving assistants was J. W. Hudston. He came from England in 1924 and died in 1937 at age eighty-five. Fr. Stanley officiated at his funeral at St. Andrew's in June of 1937.

Another assistant was the Rev. Strong from Kansas, who came to Denver to recover from tuberculosis.

Fr. Stanley and his assistants in front of the new clergy house, ca. 1928

An assistant with unusual ties to the parish was Emmett Jones. He grew up in the St. Andrew's church because his mother was the housekeeper for Fr. Stanley. Jones was ordained in 1935 after graduating from the University of Denver and General Seminary in New York. He served briefly as a curate for Fr. Stanley in 1935. He served as an Army chaplain in World War II, retiring as a lieutenant colonel. Jones died at age eighty-two in 1992. The Rev. Jones is memorialized by a 1995 plaque in the gardens to the west of the church building.

The Rev. Emmett Jones served as curate in 1935 for Fr. Stanley and later became an Army chaplain, retiring as a lieutenant colonel.

STANLEY'S POSITIONS WITHIN THE DIOCESE

Fr. Stanley was involved in various ways in the life of the Episcopal Diocese of Colorado. Early in his Denver career, he served as chaplain of St. Luke's Episcopal Hospital. Other positions included the presidency of the diocesan Clericus, chairmanship of the Board of Examining Chaplains, and a member of the Commission on Church Architecture and the Allied Arts.

The Commission on Church Architecture and the Allied Arts was established in 1921 by Marion Grace Hendrie and Elisabeth Spalding. The purpose of the commission was "to encourage and guide parishes and missions in obtaining the best possible design in buildings and furnishings."[17] The diocese also empowered the commission to take action as well as to guide. As a result, it was an influential instrument of the diocese.

Fr. Stanley was an arts advocate from the perspective of the Oxford Movement, which encouraged the expression of spirituality through the arts. Stanley's earliest efforts to bring art into St. Andrew's parish focused on sculptures of Mary, the mother of Jesus. The result was the *Gothic Virgin* and the *Byzantine Madonna*— both by sculptor Marion Buchan. In addition, the 1928 clergy house benefitted from consultation with the Commission on Church Architecture and the Allied Arts.

In 1931, the reredos by Albert Byron Olson was donated to St. Andrew's by Edwin Beard Hendrie. Hendrie originally commissioned the artwork to be placed in the brand-new St. Martin's Chapel for children (1928) of St. John's Cathedral. Hendrie paid $3,320.30 for the work. However, Olson's mural with its gold and brightly colored panels "obliterated" all the other artwork in the chapel.[18] Hendrie's decision to donate it to St. Andrew's was made during the period when Mr. Hendrie and his wife lived in Richthofen Castle together with their daughter Gertrude Hendrie Grant and her husband, William West Grant II, prominent lay leaders of the St. Andrew's parish. By donating Olson's work to St. Andrew's, the artwork remained in the family's religious domain. Hendries participated in St. John's Cathedral. Grants were members of St. Andrew's.

STANLEY THE THEOLOGIAN

On January 20, 1928, Fr. Stanley was interviewed by *The Rocky Mountain News*. He was questioned about a 1923 meeting between

17. Cuba, *Denver Artists Guild*, 120.
18. Hendrie, letter to Olson, May 2, 1930.

Roman Catholics and the Anglican Church. It was called the Malines Conversations, which Fr. Stanley carefully explained were "unofficial exchanges for the purpose of removing misunderstanding and for the comparison of positions of the two bodies."[19] The newspaper story reports on a variety of issues that Fr. Stanley discussed with the reporter. However, the headline proclaimed, "Denver Minister says Papal Supremacy is Only Issue." The newspaper quotes Stanley as saying, "Absolutely the one and only point of difference between us Anglicans and Rome is the Papacy."[20]

The newspaper also indicated that Fr. Stanley would further discuss the matter from the Anglican standpoint at the 11:00 a.m. High Mass in St. Andrew's church. And so he did.

At the same time, on Sunday, January 22, 1928, two other sermons were preached in response to the newspaper headline. One was by the Very Rev. Benjamin Dagwell, the dean of St. John's Cathedral. The other was by the Rev. R. B. H. Bell of St. Thomas Episcopal Church (Denver).

Both sermons were collected by Delphine Schmidt "for the record." The Rev. Bell's sermon presented eleven differences between Anglicans and Roman Catholics from his point of view. It was offered as a refutation of Stanley's quote in *The Rocky Mountain News* story.

Dean Dagwell was a vocal proponent of Low Church practices. Repeatedly in his sermon he took issue with the newspaper account about Fr. Stanley's quoted remarks. The longer Dagwell spoke, the more hostile his words became.

"A small group of Anglo-Catholics have banded themselves together. They have a little church here in Denver where they have resurrected many evil practices which have no place in the worship of the Protestant Episcopal Church, and are contrary to the Reformation. I do not know how their clergyman explains his vows to himself, but a little noisy church of 190 communicants does not

19. Chase, "Denver Minister."
20. Chase, "Denver Minister."

set the standard for the Protestant Episcopal Church in Colorado, which has over 11,000 communicants."[21]

Dean Dagwell went on to speak of the thirteen congregations in the diocese that were Anglo-Catholic. "Thirteen Clergymen have banded themselves into a bloc, against which no one dares raise their voice in protest . . . I don't see how they are allowed to go on doing the things which they do. So flagrantly. People who do that sort of thing must be either insane or dishonest."[22]

Quietly, just one mile from the cathedral, Fr. Stanley also preached a sermon responding to *The Rocky Mountain News* story. Ever the theologian and church history professor, he presented the historical background of church development over the centuries. "We inherit (we did not make it)—we inherit a religious state whose frontiers touch Protestantism, Orthodoxy, and Latin Catholicism."[23]

Stanley wove the story of the Anglican Church into a wider tapestry of a complex genealogy called the Christian movement. Speaking of the Roman Catholic adherence to papal authority, Stanley said, "The issue—the sole issue—is that of absolutism. We (the Anglican Church) believe external, disciplinary, absolutism—no matter how good the people administering it; no matter how much it can claim as efficiency, is inherently and essentially wrong."[24]

Using his creative preaching style, he concluded with a litany of affirmations of what Anglicans *do* profess. He ends his sermon with nine Protestant convictions. "If people will have it that we are Protestant, we might as well protest (affirm) . . ."

The last of the affirmations proclaimed, "As good Protestants, we covet the scientific and critical temper which is willing to look the matter in the face; to follow the evidence even when it leads to positions that we don't particularly like—the scientific temper that is quite ready to accept all the provisional difficulties that go with experiment and observations."[25]

21. Dagwell, sermon, January 22, 1928, 2.
22. Dagwell, sermon, January 22, 1928, 2.
23. Stanley, sermon, January 22, 1928, 2.
24. Stanley, sermon, January 15, 1933, 2.
25. Stanley, sermon, January 15, 1933, 2.

Stanley's sermon anticipated later theological developments. Anglicans have now agreed on statements on nearly every theological doctrine of the early church *except* papal supremacy. Stanley's sermon also pointed toward later theological developments by Protestant theologian Paul Tillich, who coined the term "the Protestant principle" — the principle of self-criticism by the church.

As the bringer of change into the diocese, Stanley's leadership of Anglo-Catholic liturgy and practices into the parish of St. Andrew's produced dissent as well as acceptance in Colorado and beyond. According to Will Grant, "Father Stanley spent his life envied and disliked by many of the higher clergy who were afraid of his brains, (and yet) idolized by his congregation . . . He had great influence among the younger priests of this and surrounding dioceses."[26]

STANLEY THE WRITER

Writing seemed to come naturally to Fr. Stanley. He wrote sermons, poems, short stories, adventure books, letters, and theological articles for journals. Copies of his sermons from 1926 to 1942 are preserved in bound volumes. Unbound copies from 1927 to 1939 are primarily mimeographed. After Stanley's death, three collections of his sermons on special topics were privately published in 1945–1946 by Mrs. William West Grant II (Gertrude Hendrie Grant). The topics include the Sermon on the Mount, Sermons on the Eucharist, and Sermons for the Times.

Stanley sermons seem to have elicited wide response. Some folks could not get enough and requested copies over a period of years from parishioner Delphine Schmidt, who mimeographed them and labeled them with the name of the requesting person. Gertrude Hendrie Grant's privately published sermons on special topics attracted a targeted audience.

After twenty-two years of listening to and reading Stanley sermons, the congregation was likely the most informed parish in the diocese about Anglo-Catholic historic roots and meaning. It was a match between a theologian of the church and a rapt student body.

26. Grant, *Such Is Life*, 172.

Poetry often crept into Stanley's sermons. His style of preaching incorporated classical literature—both prose and poetry. Besides quoting poets of the past, Stanley wrote his own.

In a creative blend of creed and poetry, Fr. Stanley produced a collection of poems based on the Nicene Creed. It was called *Traditio Symboli*. He took just a couple words at a time from the creed and penned a poetic response. Using the words "and was incarnate," Stanley wrote:

> Did a tiger look on him,
> > Little Jesus, as he lay?
> Did the morning star grow dim
> > To call its Maker to his play?
> Did the twilight from the west
> > Find him tired, as babies are, —
> Call the Baby God to rest,
> > Who made the tiger and the star?
>
> Did the Doctors of the Law
> > Know the Logos whom they taught;
> That the little Child they saw
> > Sustained the thinker and his thought,
> That an Infant's will had might,
> > Holding earth and heaven, the while
> Shone the Uncreated Light
> > Wistful in a young Lad's smile?[27]

Stanley's collection of poems based on the Nicene Creed was published in London, most likely during one of his summers spent in England during the 1920s or 1930s. However, the published collection did not include a date. Both the published book and typed manuscripts of *Traditio Symboli* are in the parish archives.

In 1942, Stanley's *Pleasance of Exile* was crafted from his hospital bed at Mercy Hospital in Denver. The unpublished collection of fifty-five poems was typed and preserved by Delphine Schmidt and is also in the parish archives. One of the poems is quoted in a later section of this chapter.

27. Stanley, *Traditio Symboli*, 28.

Stanley's love of poetry reflected yet another aspect of the Oxford Movement. One of the founding fathers of the Movement was the poet John Keble. Poetry was considered a vehicle of religious language and frequently used in the life of the church.

Legends abound about the adventure stories that Stanley is purported to have written. The legendary accounts indicate that Fr. Stanley used a pseudonym (or several). As Will Grant tells the story, "For recreation he wrote stories of adventure for the pulp magazines, at which he made a substantial income which he used for the church."[28]

Pulp magazines were so named because they were made from cheap wood pulp paper. The long and checkered history of these publications began in 1882 and ended with World War II, when paper became scarce. During their half-century life span, many hundreds of publishers came and went. In addition, the genres of fiction covered a wide span and included both children's and adult magazines. The varieties included topics such as horror, sports, exploitative topics, gangster, romance, trains, detective stories, science fiction, Western stories, and hero stories.

A number of twentieth-century authors published some of their initial work in pulp magazines. Among them were Stephen Crane, Earle Stanley Gardner, Zane Gray, Ray Bradbury, and Tennessee Williams. It was common to use pen names.

The popularity of pulp magazines rose dramatically in the 1920s and reached its zenith in the 1930s. During this period, Fr. Stanley typically spent summers in England. Pulp magazines thrived in England as well as the U.S. It was in London where Stanley's poetic collection of *Traditio Symboli* was published. It is conceivable that he may have had adventure stories published in England as well.

One of Stanley's literary interests that surfaced in his letters to Will Grant involved colorful characters with distinctive and humorous ways of speaking. Some of these Stanley passages were quoted in Grant's 1952 memoirs. Stanley's adventure story writing

---

28. Grant, *Such Is Life*, 170.

may have included colorful characters with unique and entertaining terms of speech.

The combination of Stanley's unknown pseudonym(s) with long-gone publishers and publications makes his adventure stories a mystery for the ages.

For similar reasons of fading publications, Fr. Stanley's contributions to religious journals of his day seem to be elusive. In his lifetime, Stanley was known as an authority on church history and ritual. In this role, he wrote articles for various religious journals. The passage of eighty to a hundred years of time seems to have obliterated their pages.

END OF LIFE FOR FR. STANLEY

By late summer of 1942, Fr. Stanley had developed cancer of the hip. His doctor was "the leading bone specialist of the region"[29] and committed his patient to Mercy Hospital in early September of that year. It was a hospital run by Catholic nuns who had a close relationship with the Sisters of St. Anne. According to Will Grant, it was also one of the leading Roman Catholic institutions of the region.

In his memoirs, Will Grant describes the story. "The members of his congregation came to see him as often as permitted, even to the extent of seeking arbitration in internecine disputes. As Fr. Stanley said to me, 'After all, this business of dying might be easier without such interruptions.'"[30]

The diocesan newspaper furthers the story. "Fr. Stanley spent much of his time during the early part of his illness supervising the affairs of his parish and the election of the new rector, the Rev. Charles D. Evans. He was constantly attended during his illness by the Rev. James L. McLane, rector of the Episcopal Church of the Ascension, Denver."[31]

---

29. Grant, *Such Is Life*, 178.
30. Grant, *Such Is Life*, 178.
31. "Death Ends 26 Years," March 1943.

At the beginning of his three-month hospitalization, Fr. Stanley wrote poems. The very first in his collection of fifty-five poems begins as follows:

FIRST VERSE:
Now gently dies the dying world away,
 And all its tireless captivating might,
And wonder dawning only yester-day,
 And loveliness begotten our last night."

LAST VERSE:
"One studied to be quiet, and as one
 Led by calm waters came on eventide
And heard a Voice annul oblivion:
 LET US PASS OVER TO THE OTHER SIDE.[32]

On September 13, 1942, he gave his collection of poems to parishioner Delphine Schmitt. She carefully typed them and preserved *The Pleasance of Exile* by Neil Stanley for the parish archives. They were never published.

On Sunday, October 25, 1942, Stanley's longtime clergy friend, the Rev. James McLane of the Episcopal Church of the Ascension, stood in the pulpit at St. Andrew's. At Fr. Stanley's request, Fr. McLane read the farewell message from the rector to his parishioners. (Fr. Stanley remained in the hospital.) The message began as follows.

> What I want you to do is to give to the new rector the same generous loyalty that you have always given to me.
>
> There are two points that I want to make—one negative—the other positive.
>
> The first is that you will show your loyalty by *never* quoting me to him. I do not want to live on as a legend that will be a nuisance. Because he is a different person, he will do things in a different way—and *that is right.*
>
> The second point is a positive one—that you will make a point, all of you, of praying daily for your new rector.

32. Stanley, *Pleasance of Exile*, 1942.

> We get as good as we deserve—and the measure of
> our deserving is the measure of prayer.[33]

In addition, Fr. Stanley asked Fr. McLane to read two passages from Bunyan's *Pilgrim's Progress*. The passages gave two different accounts of passing over the river of death. The first picture was an ideal one. The second account was the difficult one. The latter description reflected the difficult and painful death of Fr. Stanley.

> The conclusion is that as I have always prayed for you,
> where knowledge is imperfect and prayer is frequently
> mistaken, so always I shall pray for you, and shortly,
> where knowledge is complete and where prayer is om-
> nipotence of prayer.[34]

On November 30, 1942—the feast day of St. Andrew—Fr. Stanley died.

On December 1, 1942, his body laid in state at Rogers Mortuary. Fr. Stanley requested no flowers.

On December 2, 1942, from 7:30 to 9:30 a.m. Masses were said at St. Andrew's Episcopal Church.

At 10:30 a.m. Requiem Mass was held with the Rev. James L. McLane of Ascension Episcopal Church as the celebrant. The Rev. Charles D. Evans, current rector, read the Burial Office. He was assisted by Canon Harry Watts of St. John's Cathedral, a seminary classmate of Fr. Stanley's.

Cremation followed at Fairmount Cemetery.

Burial took place at St. Anne's in the Hills, where Fr. Stanley's ashes were interred next to the altar of the outdoor chapel. Bishop Fred Ingley presided. The Sisters of St. Anne kept an all-night vigil in their Denver chapel. They also held a private Requiem Mass at their Denver convent.

33. Stanley, "Farewell Message," October 25, 1942.
34. Stanley, "Farewell Message."

Fr. Stanley's original grave in 1942 was identified with the same style of marker in the shape of a cross that was used for all the sisters buried at St. Anne's in the Hills.

TRIBUTES

"In loving memory of Rev. Neil Stanley" is the inscription on the wooden wall plaque that forms the stoup (font) of holy water at St. Andrew's Episcopal Church. It is just inside the door leading to the back of the nave. No further information is given on the plaque. One possibility is that the Sisters of St. Anne, who often worked quietly and unassumingly behind the scenes, may have offered this tribute to their beloved chaplain and warden. The gift may continue as a secret of the saints.

Gertrude Hendrie Grant visited Mercy Hospital with the intention of paying the bill for Fr. Stanley's three months of care. The Catholic sister responded to her offer by saying, "We won't take a penny, Mrs. Grant, nor for the x-rays either. We know a holy man when we see one. It has done us all good to have him here."[35] The doctor responded with equal generosity.

St. Mark's Chapel, South Park, Blechingley, England, underwent considerable damage in World War II. By 1949, it was restored and renovated. "The priest's room next to the upstairs library was dedicated to the memory of the Rev. Neil Stanley."[36] The chapel is located on the estate of Mr. Uvedale Lambert, who married Melanie Grant, the daughter of William and Gertrude Grant (Denver).

In 1951, St. Andrew's dedicated a newly rebuilt Kimball organ to Fr. Stanley. The Rev. Gordon Graser, vicar, suggested the memorial, and the bishop's committee (of Bishop Harold Bowen) passed a resolution to do so.

Such Is Life, the 1952 memoirs of Will Grant, includes a chapter called "My Religious Life." It is primarily a tribute to Fr. Stanley. "So ended the life of a great priest and a holy man ... He loved God first, and then his neighbor. His example and his sermons continue to animate us."[37]

Another tribute to Fr. Stanley by Will Grant is offered in a remembrance of an early event in Stanley's ministry at St. Andrew's. Fr. Stanley invited two monks from the Order of the Holy Cross (West Park, New York) to lead a special preaching mission at St. Andrew's in 1923. Grant was particularly moved by the leader of the preaching mission, Fr. Shirley Hughson, whom Grant remembers as "the holiest man I have ever met."[38] In conclusion, Grant declares, "I do not doubt that there are holy men in other churches. As it happens, it has been my experience to know but two intimately ... Father Hughson and Father Stanley."[39]

35. Grant, *Such Is Life*, 178.
36. "Priests Room Dedicated," April 1949.
37. Grant, *Such Is Life*, 178.
38. Grant, *Such Is Life*, 171.
39. Grant, *Such Is Life*, 172.

BURIAL POSTSCRIPT

Over time, the Sisters of St. Anne shifted their focus from convalescent home to school. After 1950, their work centered on development of the St. Anne's Episcopal School. By 1967, the school governance was transferred to a board of directors. The sisters' properties on York Street in Denver and at St. Anne's in the Hills near Morrison, Colorado were repurposed for academic instruction.

In 1968, a quarter-century after Neil Stanley's death, his ashes were transferred from St. Anne's in the Hills to Riverside Cemetery in Denver. The initial resting place of Stanley's ashes next to the outdoor altar at St. Anne's in the Hills was likely no longer a central focus of devotion by the sisters.

The same grave marker from his original burial site is now in place at Riverside Cemetery. It is a small, simple marker that lays flat against the earth in the shape of a cross. It reads, "Jesu Mercy—Neil Stanley—Priest—1889–1942." (His birthdate is incorrect. He was born in 1890.) The grave marker is identical to the grave markers of the Sisters of St. Anne in the burial grounds at St. Anne's in the Hills.

Current burial site for Fr. Stanley's ashes is at the Riverside Cemetery in Denver. His ashes were transferred from St. Anne's in the Hills in 1968.

A LEGACY OVERVIEW

The Rev. Neil Stanley's legacy at St. Andrew's Episcopal Church is the heritage of the Oxford Movement. Its Anglo-Catholic liturgy and practices restored early church ritual and customs. Pastoral and moral care, including to the most vulnerable in need, marked the ministries of Oxford Movement practitioners. Artistic expression produced sculptures and altar murals and Gothic Revival design. Poetry and music found fresh forms of expression. New monastic orders emerged.

Most personally, Stanley's legacy is reflected in relationships. As recounted in this chapter, he was both pastor and friend to Will and Gertrude Grant, Delphine Schmidt, Sister Adah Gabriel, Mother Noel and Sisters of St. Anne, the Titus family, David Lyons, and many unknown to history.

"He lived the life of a saint. He was always putting boys through college and helping people. In the mornings the clergy house would be full of boys, all of whom stayed to breakfast. His residence was the center of parish activity during his lifetime."[40]

Stanley's long-time colleague Will Grant proclaimed, "Such was Father Stanley, our friend and our spiritual guide till his death. By long odds, he was the best informed and most learned theologian the church ever had in the Rocky Mountain region and one of the best anywhere."[41]

Decades after Stanley's death, a granddaughter of Will and Gertrude Grant remembers growing up in the St. Andrew's parish. Melanie Grant remarks that others "following Rev. Neil Stanley did not match Stanley's considerable intellect and spirituality."[42] Leaders who followed Stanley chartered different pathways with different goals.

Fr. Stanley himself remained wholeheartedly committed to the core visions of the Oxford Movement. In speaking of the church the day before he died, he confessed to his friend Will

---

40. Grant, *Such Is Life*, 170.
41. Grant, *Such Is Life*, 171.
42. Melanie Grant, interview, June 25, 2015.

Grant, "If there were only one Anglo-Catholic left in the world, I should be that one."[43]

DOCUMENTS CONSULTED

Ancestory.com, "Neil Edmund Stanley"
Denver city directories, 1920–1930
U.S. Census Bureau, Denver, Colorado

PEOPLE CONSULTED

Ronald Fox, assistant to the president, Bexley Seabury Seminary, Chicago

Gertie, Melanie, and Newell Grant, grandchildren of William West Grant II, Denver, Colorado

Candy Porter, historian, Charles Winfred Douglas homestead, Evergreen, Colorado

Christopher Pote, seminary archivist, Virginia Theological Seminary, Alexandria, Virginia

Gregory Robbins, chair, Religious Studies, University of Denver

Micah Saxton, head librarian, Iliff School of Theology, Denver, Colorado

John Wengrovious, historian, Episcopal Church in Colorado, Golden, Colorado

Stephen Zimmerman, historian, Anglican/Episcopal Church, Cape Coral, Florida

---

43. Grant, *Such Is Life*, 178.

3

The Rev. Jon Marr Stark

Rector of St. Andrew's Episcopal Church
1969–1984

> My imperfections and failures are as much a blessing from
> God as my successes and my talents, and I lay them both at
> his feet.
>
> —Attributed to Mahatma Gandhi

BIOGRAPHICAL BACKGROUND

In August 1933, Jon Marr Stark was born into a prominent Denver family. His father owned a local lumber company. His mother's family owned the national chain of grocery stores known as Piggley Wiggley. A sister Elaine was a year and a half older.

An uncle of Fr. Jon's, Galen Nicholas Marr, had a chronic illness as a child. The Sisters of St. Anne took care of him at their York Street residence in Denver. This is yet another example of the commitment of the Sisters of St. Anne to welcome chronically afflicted children on both a long-term and short-term basis. The family was so profoundly grateful to the sisters that they became major donors of their work. A plaque on a second-floor room of the west wing includes the name of Galen—a memorial to him and an indication of the donation from the family for the building.

Fr. Jon graduated from the University of Colorado (Boulder) in the mid-1950s with a degree in English. He was an active participant in the university's theater department. Among the students at CU Boulder during Fr. Jon's time were several young men who later became ordained into the Episcopal ministry and worked with Fr. Jon in later life. One of them was William Frey, who later served as Episcopal Bishop of Colorado (1973–1990) during the Order of the Holy Family's ministry at the St. Andrew's Abbey.

After graduating from seminary at Nashotah House (Nashotah, Wisconsin) in 1959, Fr. Jon served for nine years in Estes Park, Colorado as vicar of Saint Bartholomew's Episcopal Church. While there, he formed a coffee house ministry for young people—an emerging form of ministry among 1960s nonconforming youth, often referred to as "counterculture."

Following this ministry, he spent a year exploring life as an itinerant in Europe. Thus he experienced firsthand what it was like to "live on the road" without a home. Upon return to the United States, Fr. Jon enrolled in the Chicago Urban Training Center for further training in ministry to urban youth. Poverty of upended youth in urban areas, a call to monastic life, and the church's long history of hospitality to the stranger combined to forge a passionate vision within this thirty-six-year-old priest. In January of 1969, Fr. Jon became the rector of St. Andrew's Episcopal Church in Denver, Colorado.

CHANGE COMES TO ST. ANDREW'S PARISH

The 1960s were a decade of upheaval and fomenting ideas. The Vietnam War produced the peace movement. In addition came the civil rights movement, the farmworkers movement, the feminist movement, and the environmental movement. Societal norms were challenged. Experiments of communal living formed in both secular and religious communities.

And in a quiet block on the edge of downtown Denver, a pairing of church and society gave birth to a sanctuary in the city. It grew to be known as St. Andrew's Abbey, the home of a new religious order called The Order of the Holy Family. This fledgling ministry of hospitality came into being on June 29, 1969. For the first few years, the new creation explored how to be a haven for those seeking refuge from life on the streets of Denver. It was often hit or miss. Initial instability evolved into a structure and its ministries continued for a total of fifteen years.

Fr. Jon invited a major religious order of the Episcopal Church to come to Denver, investigate possibilities, and consider beginning a foundation. In response, a monk was dispatched to investigate. However, the religious order decided that Denver was "not a place where a foundation would flourish."[1]

In Fr. Jon's words, "Still an Order was developing, and it was about to overtake the rector."[2]

1. Stark, *Men Athirst for God*, 3.
2. Stark, *Men Athirst for God*, 3.

WHO WERE THE GUESTS SEEKING HELP?

Brother Paul with counterculture young people at St. Andrew's Abbey, ca. 1970

In the beginning (1969–1971), the majority of guests were from the counterculture group known as "crashers," "hippies," "transients," or those "on the road." They carried backpacks and the impulse to travel freely. Others in those beginning years were runaways who were also "on the road" to escape negative circumstances. In the early 1970s, hundreds of runaways were reconciled with their families through the intervention of the Order of the Holy Family.

Brother Francis Joachim with a young runaway, ca. 1970

The United States did not have youth hostels like Europe. Therefore, for youth stranded in Denver on their cross-country road trip, St. Andrew's became a beacon of hospitality. Fr. Jon described "being inundated by hundreds of young people. And they were asking to be fed, and housed, and counseled, and directed to doctors and lawyers, and sometimes just to a phone so they could call home."[3] In 1969–1971, these overnight guests numbered roughly one thousand a month. Somewhere around five thousand meals a month were served to them in the parish crypt. The young travelers were given free meals and lodging for three days. After that, they were asked to pay twenty-five cents a meal. Most "on the road" travelers did not stay three days.

To serve their additional needs, the clergy house was transformed into the Safe House. The common room was boarded off

3. Stark, *Men Athirst for God*, 3.

from the rest of first floor to provide the private Crisis Control Center. Services included storage for backpacks, mail and messages, twenty-four-hour emergency telephone service, free legal referrals, and a nationwide directory of counterculture services. A rapidly growing number (around forty) of volunteer professionals staffed the Safe House and the fast-growing healthcare facilities. Included were doctors, lawyers, nurses, and medical technicians. Members of the Order of the Holy Family also worked in the Safe House.

Some parishioners responded to this crush of visitors by reordering their typical workday schedule. On their way to work, they came to early morning Mass and then helped prepare breakfast for the young travelers. After work, they returned to help prepare an evening meal followed by assisting in bedding down the travelers for the night.

In this unusual and groundbreaking sanctuary of hospitality, a new ministry was being formed by a young rector with a vision, a handful of parishioners, fledgling monks and nuns, professional volunteers, and a growing stream of youthful visitors with a long list of needs.

Denver's young street population in the 1970s reflected a complex mixture of diverse needs. In addition to those "on the road," a number were outcasts from the healthcare system. Some suffered from mental illness; others from alcohol or drug addictions; others from sex exploitation; and some were former prison inmates. Therefore, initial ministries of food, overnight shelter, and the Crisis Control Center were not sufficient to meet the wide range of needs.

EXPANDING INTO THE NEIGHBORHOOD

1971

To accommodate its mushrooming ministries, the abbey leased three row houses on Twenty-Second Avenue—two blocks away. They were known as The Annex. The eastern-most dwelling housed the sisters. The middle house was the Dr. William D. Millett Memorial Free Clinic at 828 East Twenty-Second Avenue. The Free Clinic evolved from a one-room facility to five rooms and doubled as overnight sleeping quarters for women guests. The western-end house provided an overflow unit for the abbey and one guest room. (Note: Men guests were housed in the main church building on Glenarm Place. Women guests were housed in The Annex.)

Dr. Ken Osgood (left), Sister Clare, and Fr. Jon at the William D. Millett Memorial Free Clinic at 828 East Twenty-Second Avenue, ca. 1971

1975

During the expansive years of the 1970s, another facility was acquired at 851 East Eighth Avenue in the fall of 1975. It was known as Prodigal House and provided short-term (for a few weeks) emotional-behavioral care for runaways and youth in crisis. Its professional staff worked with the courts and social service agencies.

1977

In June 1977, the Order of the Holy Family further expanded its ministries to a mountain retreat center near Steamboat Springs, Colorado, which they purchased and named The Lichen. It served as a long-term residential treatment center offering emotional-behavioral care. The Lichen Institute was accredited by the University of Denver. Within its first year, The Lichen was serving twenty patients.

The Lichen was a long-term residential treatment center for adolescent emotional/behavioral care located near Steamboat Springs, Colorado, ca. 1977.

Originally the property was an executive retreat for Phillips Petroleum, with its Rabbit Ears Lodge built in the 1950s.

Immediately next door to the south of the clergy house was the Carpenter's Union building. The Order of the Holy Family used the Union building for job training in printing, offered by the A. B. Dick Company. Another job training program in cooking was housed in the abbey kitchen. Job training was one of the many services the abbey provided for homeless youth.

In the abbey's waning years (1980–1984), the Carpenter's Union event center hosted a community Thanksgiving dinner for the homeless. Current parishioner Judie James participated in this event, which was cosponsored by other community services. A hotel, for example, provided the turkeys. Judie remembers baking two dozen pies for the occasion.

THE ORDER OF THE HOLY FAMILY

As the ministry to young persons on the street developed, a monastic order was rapidly forming under the leadership of Fr. Jon. Its wide-ranging members included men, women, and a married couple. As Fr. Jon described it, "From this beginning, the Order just sort of grew."[4]

On August 31, 1974, the feast day of St. Aidan, the Order of the Holy Family was formally established. Colorado bishop the Rt. Rev. William Frey regularized the order in accordance with the canons of the Episcopal Church. Fr. Jon, who was renamed Fr. Jon Aidan, was blessed as the abbot of the order.

The name of the newly formed order reflects New Testament scripture. A central teaching of Jesus is found in Matthew 25:35–36: "For I was hungry and you gave me food, I was thirsty and you gave me something to drink, I was a stranger and you welcomed me, I was naked and you gave me clothing . . ." Continuing in verse 40: "Truly I tell you, just as you did it to one of the least of these who are members of my family, you did it unto me" (NRSV). Fr. Jon interpreted this passage by saying that the Holy Family becomes visible when these basic needs are provided by a community of love and service to others.

In 1975, the Order of the Holy Family began one of its most unique innovations. It formed the Donatus Brother Program. Unsettled young men were invited to "live as temporary members of the monastic community, to share in the prayer, work, and

4. Brother Michael, "Strangers in Town," 6.

fellowship of the community, and acquire job training and some living skills necessary to today's complex world."[5]

Fr. Jon describes the Donati Brothers as "representatives of a neglected portion of society. Some are recently divorced or plagued by alcoholism or drug experiences; some have been inmates of prisons or mental hospitals, while others have been victimized by big-city sex exploitation."[6] They ranged from ages eighteen to thirty.

Their monastic habit consisted of blue jeans plus hip-length dark blue denim tunics with a white girdle (rope around the waist) and bells on the end. They wore a small crucifix. They received job training in the abbey kitchen or the A. B. Dick print shop. They also worked in the garden or engaged in laundry or cleaning.

STRETCHING THE WALLS OF CHURCH AND RECTOR

The clergy house (rectory) was used for living space of the brothers. The abbot's quarters consisted of a small room next to the Glenarm Place front door. Many of the current second-floor rooms were divided in half to form cells for the brothers. The kitchen quarters at the back of the building were set up to serve large quantities of food. An industrial-style stove was in place. The current common room was sealed off from the rest of first floor and housed the Safe House Crisis Center during the 1970s. At the very beginning and very end of the abbey years, the current office space was used as a dining room. Laundry facilities occupied the basement.

The current Undercroft of the main church building was known as the crypt. It provided both dining room space for meals and sleeping spaces overnight.

YOUNG PEOPLE WHO VISITED THE ABBEY

The most compelling stories of the St. Andrew's Abbey years are told by the young guests who came to the abbey for help. Following

5. Stark, *Men Athirst for God*, 10–11.

6. Hodges, "Brothers Help City's Needy."

are two stories illustrating the wide range of circumstances of the young people.

A Runaway Restored to Home in 1969

Twelve-year-old Richie Pardo encountered the Brothers by word-of-mouth in 1969. Young Richie had run away from his Chicago home to California. As he hitch-hiked his way along the California coast, he was picked up by the state patrol, placed on an airplane bound for Chicago, and ended up as a seatmate of the editor of the Boulder, Colorado *Free Press*.

"I'm getting off in Denver," the editor told the young runaway. "Why don't you get off with me and check out the St. Andrew's Abbey in downtown Denver?" Richie was persuaded. He got off the plane, took a bus downtown, and made his way to the Abbey. At this time (1969), the Abbey had barely begun, yet was making an impact.

"It was an incredible experience," the 60-year-old Richie exclaims today. "For the first time in my life, I had a support system." Young Richie lived in an apartment with Brother Francis Joachim. During the daytime, everyone at the Abbey shared in cleaning and assorted tasks—including Richie. The Brothers maintained regular prayers and the discipline of overnight silence. In their worship, chanting was often a cappella or with guitar or other instruments.

Communal meals around the large dining room table took place in the adjacent rectory. Richie particularly remembers the elk meat donated to the Abbey for one of the meals.

Richie and Brother Francis Joachim connected, bonded, and worked well together. Their ongoing interaction blended together "helpful counseling" and their mutual interests of jazz music. "It helped enormously!" Richie remembers. "The truth helped me persevere. It meant a lot."

The days melded into weeks. And slowly Richie gained a different perspective. Brother Francis Joachim also served as a mediator, talking by telephone with Richie's family. Eventually Richie returned to his parental home in Chicago.

Reflecting on his life changing experience with the Brothers of the Holy Family, Richie also affirms the direct influence of Brother Francis Joachim on Richie's musical development. In 1969 Richie was learning to play the piano. Brother Francis Joachim introduced Richie to jazz. Richie is currently a jazz bass player; sometimes jazz cello. He organized Richie's Pardo Quintet which performs with bass, cello, saxophone, piano, and drums. The group has long been a staple in the Chicago area and has made several recordings.

Richie and his wife have owned the Webster Street Picture Frame Company in Chicago for nearly thirty years. Their son Ben Pardo lives in Boulder, Colorado where he is a computer teacher.

In deep gratitude for the gift of a transformed life, Richie pays high tribute to the Brothers of the St. Andrew's Abbey. "I loved the message they always gave. Love."[7]

Mental Illness and Addiction in 1975

Mark walked in the back gate a few days ago. It was the first time we had seen him on his feet since he left here in the arms of two policemen in April. Currently he was trembling with nervousness and the exertion of walking the twelve blocks from the Basic Care Home in which he had been lodged since he was released from the Psychiatric Ward of Denver General Hospital. His arm was still in a cast as a result of a leap from a third-story window in an attempt to escape from the hospital.

In Denver General Hospital, he had received little or no psychiatric therapy or counseling. Instead, he had

7. Kester, "Transformed Life," 20–21.

been placed by Welfare in a Basic Care Home, and he had been kept sedated with Heldal, one of the butyro-phenones, which is used to soothe agitation, hostility, and hallucinations.[8]

In the same issue of *The Famlian* was a lengthy letter from the parents of this young man named Mark. It recounted the horrors of the family's experiences—trying to live with the mental illness and violence of their son, who was addicted to a combination of LSD and other drugs.

In succeeding editions of *The Famlian*, additional stories were published about young people who visited the abbey. Stories described the agonies of a violent alcoholic, another who was withdrawn, silent, and deeply troubled, and a gay black man who was torn between two worlds of hope and hopelessness.

These direct and vivid accounts of young people on the streets of Denver were also accompanied by equally vivid accounts of healthcare facilities that were significantly unequipped to handle the patients in their care. In fact, some of the facilities, such as Fr. Logan and Colorado Psychiatric Hospital, were referring patients in their twenties and thirties to St. Andrew's Abbey. As a result, the abbey established both short-term and long-term treatment centers for emotional-behavioral health issues.

TRANSFORMATION OF THE NAVE

Besides the name change of the parish from St. Andrew's Episcopal Church to a name describing the household of the Order of the Holy Family—St. Andrew's Abbey—the buildings themselves also underwent transformation.

8. Brother Irenaeus, *Famlian*, 2.

Two of the shrines during the Order of the Holy Family
honored St. Mary and St. Andrew.

The nave in the main church building included four shrines:
1) St. Mary, 2) St. Andrew, 3) St. Francis, and 4) St. Nicholas. Stations of the Cross were contributed by Brother Francis. They were
ivory-like and quite small, measuring seven inches by seven inches.
Monastic stalls along the north side of the nave indicated special
seating for the brothers of the order. The stalls were given to the Order of the Holy Family by the Order of the Holy Cross (West Park,
New York.) They were carved in a previous century by Franciscan
monks for the Queen of Missions monastery in Santa Barbara,
California.

At the back of the nave stood a large decorative rood screen
with locked doors. Its purpose was to prevent intruders from entering the nave and stealing artwork—common occurrences in the
long decades when church doors were routinely open and unlocked
during the daytime. Unfortunately, intruders climbed over the rood
screen and continued stealing artwork and sometimes furnishings
like chairs.

Brother Francis designed the iron rood screen with two lan-
terns hanging inside it. (They were also stolen.) The abbot's aunt

Mary Marr paid for the elegant screen. It was dismantled when the abbey ended its tenure in 1984.

Rood screen at back of nave, ca. 1980, with monks observing Compline at end of day

The confessional booth from the ministry of the Rev. Neil Stanley (1920–1942) remained at the back of the nave in the beginning years of the abbey. Confessions of the brothers were heard by a retired priest who served as chaplain for the occasions. In the early 1970s, the confessional was taken apart. In its place was installed a shrine of the Prodigal Child. In addition to sculpture, the shrine included a triptych made by Brother Francis.

Because of the style of worship that the brothers practiced, a freestanding altar was created by using the baptismal font with a flat cover. It was at the front of the nave on the main floor, just in front of the chancel steps. Within the chancel was the organ plus the high altar against the west wall. Worshippers were seated in pews that encircled the freestanding altar on the main floor of the nave.

The narthex was renamed the Court of the Gentiles. The term originated in biblical times when non-Jews were allowed into a designated outer portion of the temple in Jerusalem, known as the Court of the Gentiles. In monastic houses, this entrance area was for nonmembers of the religious order.

Perhaps the most prominent transformation was the chancel arch. In the original church building of 1908, the chancel arch was sizeable. This large "hanging canvas" separated the chancel from the nave. It seemed to lend itself naturally to mural art. So in 1970 Russ Stevenson painted a mural on the chancel arch. He titled his work *Breaking Away*.

Chancel mural called *Breaking Away* was painted by Russ Stevenson in 1970.

In 1977 Brother Francis painted a different mural, which he called *The Majestras*. It depicted Christ in the center top surrounded by a total of two dozen figures. Roughly half the figures were well-loved saints of the ancient church. Another half were disciples. Also tucked into the pantheon were vignettes of the Annunciation, the Visitation, and the Nativity.

St. Andrew's circa 1980

Chancel mural called *The Majestras* **was painted by Brother Francis in 1977.**

By the time of the Rev. Kenneth Near's ministry (1986–1991), the roof of the nave leaked water, which significantly damaged the mural. During the 1988 renovation of the parish buildings, local historian and architect Gary Long chose to preserve the remaining mural with epoxy before repainting the chancel arch. His thinking was that future parishioners might want to see the remnants of *The Majestras* underneath the paint. However, by the time of the 2008 expansion and remodeling, this story was essentially unknown. Therefore, the original chancel arch was removed along with the invisible, damaged mural—with most parishioners unaware of the historical art remnant that held prominence within the St. Andrew's Abbey.

Paintings also graced the walls of the nave and chancel in the abbey years. A large oil painting was known as *The Sorrowful Mother*. It was on a chancel wall directly behind the organ, next to the entry to the garth. Another painting depicted a santos. A portrait of Saint Jerome was displayed in the front of the nave.

A piece of porcelain art was embedded in another wall of the nave. Brother Francis gave a Mexican penitent crucifix, which was twenty-eight inches high and fourteen inches wide. It too was apparently stolen.

Increasing furnishings and people led to a need for expanded facilities. The abbot requested that Brother Francis draw up architectural drawings for a proposed expansion of the property. One of the essential components of the drawings was provision for housing of the sisters of the order. The dream plans did not materialize but offered a vision of what might have been.

PEOPLE WHO SERVED WITHIN THE MONASTERY

Wide-ranging ministries involve many people. At the core of St. Andrew's Abbey were the monks. Over the fifteen years of the monastery, numerous men, young people, and a few women participated. Some are listed below with known dates and special roles they played.

Abbot

Jon Aidan (Jon Marr Stark)

Brothers

Francis Joachim (1969–1972)—jazz composer and musician

Dunstan (1980–1984)—organist

Paul (1972)—editor of *Dialog* magazine

Ned (1972)

Gregory (1972)

Francis (Willard Shaw) (1972–1980)—the artist-in-residence for the order

Nicholas (1978)—editor of weekly *Famlian*

Historic Church Serves Big City

Irenaeus—editor of weekly *Famlian*; initiated inclusion of St. Andrew's Episcopal Church in the National Register of Historic Places (1975)
Seraphim (Charles Niblett Hoffacre) (1980–1984)
Boniface (Tom Rowland) (1980–1984)
Anthony (David Brewer) (1980–1984)

Sisters

Clare (1972)
Bernadette (1972)

Married Couple

John and Anna Powell (lived in a separate apartment)

Donati Brothers (young guests who temporarily served with the brothers)

Ignatius
Michael
Matthew Odney
Steve Crouche
Peter Gross

Third-Order (Lay) Member

Larry Bradford (1982)

Four monks worship within monastic stalls in the nave.

PROCESS OF BECOMING A
MEMBER OF THE ORDER

Monastic membership involved four stages. The first stage was called the "postulancy." It lasted four weeks. The postulant presented a letter of intention that described his/her reasons for desiring membership. They engaged in assigned tasks and attended all religious functions. The second stage was known as the "novitiate," which lasted two years and included formal studies similar to a seminary curriculum. Vows were required at this stage by the Holy Family. The third stage was called "junior profession" and lasted three years. During this stage, the junior members were clothed with the habit of the order, consisting of a long, blue denim garment with white girdle (rope around the waist), and white scapular (cape) and pelisse (long cloak). The final stage was named "life profession"—the full-fledged monk. Their white habit included a peace cross medallion.

Hoods were worn during periods of silence and prayer. The monks typically wore their hoods during Compline at the end of the day. They sang in front of the shrine to Mary and recessed from the nave to their cells on the second floor of the clergy house.

ACTIVITIES OF THE ABBEY

Monastic discipline formed the framework of each day. It began with the Rising Bell at 6:30 a.m. It ended at 10:00 p.m. with the Grand Silence, which continued until 6:30 the next morning.

Its traditional schedule of prayer used the *Book of Common Prayer* for its six daily offices plus one Mass. Four of the six offices were always sung. So was the Sunday Mass and all feast days. In addition, the monks observed sixteen hours a day in silence and all day on Fridays.

Throughout each day, monastic members engaged in household work of cleaning, cooking, and street patrols by pairs of monks walking in designated areas of downtown Denver to connect with young people in search of basic needs. Some monks contributed to the monastery magazine, called *Dialog*, or the weekly publication *The Famlian*. Others worked directly with the constant flow of guests arriving with questions and myriads of needs.

Monks share street patrol duty on Broadway Street, Denver in early 1970s.

When St. Andrew's Episcopal Church reached its centennial year of 1974, Brother Irenaeus worked through the tedious process of applying for the special designation of inclusion in the National Register of Historic Places. He interviewed long-time parish members and delved into historical books and periodicals. His work succeeded. St. Andrew's was placed on the National Register in 1975.

A LOVE MASS

A distinctive form of worship developed to serve the counterculture guests. It was described by Brother Michal from the Order of the Holy Cross (West Park, New York), who visited St. Andrew's Abbey in 1971.

> Participants in the Love Mass were identified as "housewives, factory workers, businessmen, maidenly aunts, a runaway's parents, heads, and smack freaks. Everyone finds out they're human beings needing each other. There is communication and that's really a turn on."
>
> Sunday night. It was dark inside the church except for the soft light from the many candles on the altar and shrines. Most people were on the floor surrounding the altar in the middle of the church. People smiled at each other. The Love Mass was about to begin. Everyone was ready.
>
> Father Jon had quietly slipped in and was sitting on the floor in front of the altar. As the Celebrant, he began talking quietly, setting the mood and stating the theme of the Love Mass. We were to center our worship around loneliness and belonging as the theme.
>
> There was a quiet folk tune hymn and then a freeform prayer. There were three readings: the first was a secular selection. The Gospel was read and then Father Jon sat down and began the dialogue sermon. A number of people added their observations and comments before Father Jon wrapped up the discussion in a sensitive summary. The intercessions were completely free and informal. The petitions and thanksgiving began to swell as concerns were verbalized.

Historic Church Serves Big City

I wasn't prepared for the offertory. The usual elements were presented on the altar and a collection was taken. Then the love basket was passed through the congregation and I could see a pair of shoes, boots, and articles of clothing heaped up and overflowing the sides. A brief prayer of thanksgiving, and then everything was distributed to those who were in need. Notes and poetry were also placed in the basket and then left on the altar.

The most impressive and unusual moment in the Love Mass is the Jesu chant, which begins with a low drone and builds into a free-form melody and harmony using only the vowel sounds of the name Jesu. We stood and locked our arms together as the incense filled the church from two thuribles and the bells hanging from the rope girdles of the brothers and sisters added their joyful sound to the chant. The prayer of consecration was intoned above the music of the Jesu chant. Then the consecration and chant ended and we all embraced each other in the Peace. The Communion followed and a final thanksgiving acclamation and dismissal sent us out in the street rejoicing.[9]

BLENDING ABBEY AND PARISH

Abbot Jon Aidan (Jon Marr Stark) held two positions. He was the abbot for the Order of the Holy Family as well as the rector of the St. Andrew's parish. Some of his work as rector is recorded in the parish register for 1932–2000 (vol. 3.) Fr. Jon, the rector, recorded three deaths from 1978 to 1981. Two of the recorded deaths were parishioners. One was an abby guest being served by the Prodigal House.

Fr. Jon originated the first columbarium of the parish. It made use of the free-standing altar consisting of the baptismal font covered with a flat top. Three departed loved ones were the first to have their ashes inurned within the altar. Parishioner John David Titus died January 17, 1978. Parishioner James Frederick Kenner died January 5, 1979. Abbey guest Jeanette "Eileen" West died January 1, 1981.

9. Brother Michael, "Strangers in Town," 9–10.

Fr. Jon's successor, Fr. Kenneth Near (1986–1991), continued the columbarium tradition. During the 1988 renovation, the high altar was dislodged from the wall and became a free-standing altar. A columbarium was constructed within the high altar. Then the ashes were transferred from the baptismal font to the high altar.

Parishioner Judith James reported in conversation with this author that in the early 1980s several different brothers served as senior wardens of the vestry.

Judith also remembers Fr. Jon's Great Dane, Bartholomew, who was called Bart. The well-behaved dog sat at his master's feet during worship services and processed with him to and from the altar. Fr. Jon's passion for animals led to four or five cats housed in the abbey. Each cat was named after a saint.[10]

CHURCH-WORLD INTERACTION

A perennial challenge for the church comes from generational and societal divides. During the 1970s, the church faced the counterculture challenge of the younger generation.

One of the ways the Order of the Holy Family addressed this challenge was through its publications. Its monthly magazine, called *Dialogue*, was edited by Brother Paul. He wrote, "For too long a time, very little dialogue has existed between the 'straight' community and the people of the counterculture. Misconceptions have been formed about street people because deaf ears turned to what 'hippies' have to say, which may not be representative of the current counterculture scene."[11]

The monthly *Dialogue* magazine was a joint publication of the Order of the Holy Family and St. Andrew's Church. It published poetry, essays, and artwork of street people and by members of the blended community of monastery and parish. Its aim was to provide a forum of communication between the wider society (including the church) and the counterculture.

10. Judith James, interview, August 17, 2016.

11. Brother Michael, "Strangers in Town," 11.

Another publication was the weekly *Famlian*. The title means "tales of the family." It provided heartrending stories about the wide spectrum of guests who visited the abbey. It also provided insight into artwork of the brothers (e.g., *The Majestras* mural of the chancel arch). The weekly stories were distributed by subscription and within St. Andrew's Abbey and parish.

Also bridging the gap between counterculture and society was the Crisis Control Center, known as the Safe House. "Part of a growing network of switchboards, trained Brothers and Sisters of the Holy Family and associates through the Free Clinic man the phones, taking calls ranging from jobs, legal aid, draft help, drug abuse to threats of suicide and the hysterical parents of runaways."[12] The center literally connected wayfarers from the street to direct resources provided by the wider society. Professionals from legal and medical backgrounds were among the volunteers who staffed the Safe House services.

"Estimating as many as 300 calls a week, Crisis Control operators must be ready to make medical and psychiatric referrals, offer information on birth control and pregnancy problems, community events, transportation, and draft or military problems. St. Andrew's is often the first number people will call when they have been injured on the road or arrested, and need help."[13]

One of the youthful guests of the St. Andrew's Abbey summarized her feelings about the services. "Safe House provides something more than just shelter: acceptance, respect, and a family-like alternative to the crash-pad scene. And it's a no-hassle thing."[14]

NIGHT VISITORS

Out of the blue on Saturday, July 24, 1971, St. Andrew's Abbey was raided by law enforcement shortly after 4:00 a.m. The church property was surrounded by a Special Services Unit accompanied by dogs, agents of the Denver Narcotics, Identification and Intelligence

12. Brother Michael, "Strangers in Town," 11.

13. Brother Michael, "Strangers in Town," 11–12.

14. Brother Michael, "Strangers in Town," 6.

bureaus, the Delinquency Control Division, and Robbery and Burglary details.

Meanwhile, two police officers with an arrest warrant pried open a screen from a rectory window, where eighty to a hundred young men were sound asleep inside. The warrant was given to the curate, the Rev. Chauncey Shaw. (The abbot, Fr. Jon, was in Evergreen, Colorado at a church conference.) The search warrant focused on guns and drugs.

The upshot resulted in approximately forty young people being arrested. None were charged. All were released. Police found a small amount of narcotics and one rifle.

Just as swiftly, response came from throughout the city of Denver. Foremost was the rector of the parish/abbot of the monastery, Fr. Jon. Expressing his initial outrage, he said he was "deeply disturbed . . . that law enforcement . . . acted against one of the most dedicated drug abuse centers in Denver."[15]

Fr. Jon was also swift to report the long-standing rule of the abbey: no drugs, no weapons. When drugs were found, they were immediately confiscated and placed in a locked desk in the abbot's quarters. Eventually they were flushed down the toilet. A rifle was once discovered in a laundry room by one of the brothers. At the abbot's direction, the rifle was placed in hiding until the owner could be found. Once found, the owner was asked to leave.

Equally swiftly, the Episcopal bishop of Colorado, the Rt. Rev. Edwin Thayer, responded. "Because of the unusual environment in which it finds itself, its opportunity is unique and therefore, open to misunderstanding. St. Andrew's has the ear of many transient and troubled youngsters and is exerting its influence in expressing the love of our Lord for them."[16]

Support within the wider church included an assortment of religious organizations. Among them were Catholics for a Better Society, the Roman Catholic Archdiocesan Sisters' Council, Northwest Youth Ministry (Roman Catholic), First Unitarian Church, and American Friends Service Committee.

15. "St. Andrew's Rector," July 25, 1971.

16. Brother Michael, "Strangers in Town," 11.

Legal action promptly responded to the raid. Maxwell Aley, a parishioner of St. Andrew's, served as an attorney for the community of parish and monastery. He and four other attorneys immediately filed a petition in Denver District Court.

"The district attorney's office initiated a series of meetings with police and high-level church officials aimed at reaching a compromise under which programs for alienated youth could continue to operate."[17]

Consequently, two developments brought positive change. 1) Safe House was authorized by the police department as a shelter for runaway youth. Collaborative action between police and parish/monastery resulted. 2) St. Andrew's formed a permanent liaison committee to promote better communications with the police.

Widespread criticism of police action increased within the city following the raid. Fr. Jon reported that "There have been people coming to the church, calling on the phone, and writing letters. Attendance at the Sunday Masses has nearly doubled."[18]

FUNDING OF THE ORDER OF THE HOLY FAMILY

This extraordinary experiment in monastic life and ministry was funded in diverse ways. It was financed separately from the operations of the St. Andrew's parish.

The Order of the Holy Family was supported, instead, by a variety of sources. Early in its operation (1970,) the order received financial assistance from the executive council of the Episcopal diocese. The council briefly provided start-up support from its experimental ministries special funding.

Many donations —large and small—came from throughout Denver and surrounding area. Food donations were made by several Denver distributors. Speaking engagements were another opportunity for income. Later in the order's life (1980), replicas of the Donati brothers' tunics were offered for sale in the original denim, or velour, or satin in a variety of color choices.

17. Brother Michael, "Strangers in Town," 11.
18. Brother Michael, "Strangers in Town," 11.

Underlying the external sourcing of the order was the internal funding provided by the abbot himself and his family. Fr. Jon's inheritance and his mother's side of the family—particularly his aunt Mary Marr—provided significant resources for the developing order. Fr. Jon indicated that "Either we're underfunded or over-programmed, and I really suspect it is both."[19]

THE WINDING DOWN OF THE ORDER OF THE HOLY FAMILY

Over the fifteen years of ministries of the St. Andrew's Abbey, a range of issues impacted the order. Differences of ideas contributed both vitality and conflict. Vision abounded along with profound convictions propelling service to those in need. At the same time, organizational structure and financial foundations floundered. Winds of change brought new dilemmas. In short, the experiment did not survive the test of time.

In the summer of 1984, Fr. Jon was treated to at least three celebrations of his ministries by parishioners and other Denver supporters. They were bidding farewell to both rector and abbot. The little parish on the edge of downtown had roughly two dozen members in 1984. The Order of the Holy Family consisted of two members: Fr. Jon and another brother who relocated to Santa Fe, New Mexico.

A LEGACY IN TIME AND SPACE

The legacy of the St. Andrew's Abbey carries a significant footprint. Its pioneering ministries to young people on the streets of Denver are continued in the services of Denver's Urban Peak. Its experiments in short-term and long-term mental healthcare for neglected urban youth are reflected in emerging Denver health agencies offering such critical services. During its lifetime, the Order of the Holy Family was invited to send a contingent of five monks to El Paso, Texas to run a drug treatment center sponsored by St. Alban's

19. Brother Michael, "Strangers in Town," 12.

Episcopal Church. In the twenty-first century, a former runaway guest at the abbey, Richie Pardo, has reconnected with the abbot and St. Andrew's parish to share his story of transformation provided by the Order of the Holy Family in 1969. On the threshold of the sesquicentennial of the St. Andrew's parish, the congregation continues to wrestle with the question of how to provide sanctuary in the city.

PEOPLE CONSULTED

Barbara Benedict, reporter and editor, *Colorado Episcopalian*, 1963–1993

Brother Francis, Order of the Holy Family, 1972–1980

William C. Frey, Episcopal Bishop of Colorado, 1973–1990

Judith James, parishioner, St. Andrew's Episcopal Church, 1980–present

the late Hal Lycett, 1959 classmate of Fr. Jon, Nashotah House Seminary

Kenneth Near, vicar, St. Andrew's Episcopal Church, 1986–1991

Merrie Need, historian, St. Anne's Episcopal School, Denver

Richard Palmer, 1959 classmate of Fr. Jon, Nashotah House Seminary

Richie Pardo, guest, Order of the Holy Family, 1969

Marge Ruby, wife of organist Hank Ruby, who served during Fr. Jon's tenure (Hank Ruby was a classmate of Fr. Jon at University of Colorado.)

John Wengrovious, Colorado Episcopal Church historian, Golden, Colorado

the late Bert Womack, canon to the ordinary during Bishop Frey's tenure (1973–1990)

4

Transitional Chapter of Repurposing and Restoring Church Buildings

1984–1986

MONASTERY YEARS

From 1969 to 1984, St. Andrew's Episcopal Church underwent a transformation. It became the home of the Order of the Holy Family—a brand new Episcopal religious order. The building became St. Andrew's Abbey as the official residence of the Order of the Holy Family. Its ministries focused on serving young people living on the streets of Denver. At the same time, the parish continued under the rector, the Rev. Jon Marr Stark. The rector served a dual role as rector of the parish and abbot of the religious order until his leave-taking in the summer of 1984.

During this innovative chapter in the history of St. Andrew's Episcopal Church, the congregation and the building turned a corner. The congregation diminished in numbers. The building suffered from deferred maintenance.

REPURPOSING THE PARISH

In late 1984, the Episcopal Bishop of Colorado, the Rt. Rev. William Frey, appointed the Rev. Dr. Cecil Franklin to serve as an interim priest. Doctor Franklin was a professor of religious studies at the University of Denver—a full-time position. His new appointment was a part-time job.

Dr. Cecil Franklin served as interim priest 1984–1986.

Parishioner Judith James remembers this time with fond memories of Dr. Franklin. "He was extremely generous with his time. At Thanksgiving, he and his wife hosted twenty parishioners in their home."[1] The congregation included a handful of parishioners—somewhere between one and two dozen.

Uncertainty of the future was the hallmark of late 1984 through 1986. Decades later, the Rev. Jon Marr Stark affirmed that "Judith James was a stable rod of strength as senior warden at this time. Without Judith, the parish would not have survived."[2]

1. Judith James, interview, August 17, 2016.
2. Jon Marr Stark (aka Jon Aidan Marr), interview, October 29, 2016.

Parishioner Judith James served as senior warden during the transition period, 1984–1986.

Approaching retirement age in 1985, Dr. Franklin acknowledged that "I'll hold the operation together until the bishop decides he wants a man with more energy."[3] Although Dr. Franklin conducted a weekly Bible study, he indicated that "we don't have enough to put on a Sunday School."[4]

Dr. Franklin produced a brochure for distribution outside the parish. He described the context of the little downtown parish along with the 10:30 Sunday morning worship. "St. Andrew's Episcopal Church is located near the meeting point of three distinct parts of Denver—Curtis Park, Capitol Hill, and downtown. The church is six blocks north of the state capitol."[5]

Continuing with a description of the immediate neighborhood, Dr. Franklin pointed out that "within a five-block radius, there are rich people, poor people, and middle-class people; black, white, brown, and yellow; families, and individuals without a family. St. Andrew's wants all of these to feel welcome to come into its family."[6]

3. Culver, "Disparate Groups."
4. Culver, "Disparate Groups."
5. Franklin, *Saint Andrew's*, 1.
6. Franklin, *Saint Andrew's*, 1.

During this transitional era, three groups from the Episcopal diocese found a home at St. Andrew's. The Episcopal Pastoral Center was a diocesan umbrella organization working with various groups to provide food, clothing, and other services to the growing population of urban poor. The Pastoral Center moved its office to the undercroft of St. Andrew's. It also provided money to pay for St. Andrew's utility and repair bills. In addition, discretionary funds from Bishop Frey and the diocese contributed to St. Andrew's upkeep. The Pastoral Center was directed by the canon to the ordinary of the diocese, the Rev. Canon Bert Womack. Eventually this group evolved into the St. Francis Day Center for homeless guests at 2323 Curtis Street in Denver.

A second group was Central Denver Community Services—later named Metro Caring—which focused on food distribution to Denver's urban poor. It also moved its offices and counseling rooms to St. Andrew's undercroft. Its food bank was housed in the clergy house. The common room of the clergy house served as their staff meeting area. Alice Stark was the director. The group was affiliated with the diocese as a city-wide ecumenical organization.

Central Denver Community Services was one of three social service agencies with offices at St. Andrew's Episcopal Church during the transition period of 1984–1986.

Thirdly, the Episcopal Inner City Church was an experimental mission of the diocese. Its vicar was the Rev. Kay Ryan, ordained May 2, 1981, the first woman to be ordained a priest in the Colorado Episcopal diocese. Its Sunday worship services were conducted at noon at St. Andrew's. The host parish of St. Andrew's worshipped at 10:30 on Sunday mornings. Both worship services were held in the clergy house common room. The sister congregation also contributed financially to St. Andrew's upkeep.

A fourth group was The Enablers—later called The Caring Connection. It was a nonprofit that provided networking services for emergency service providers. They took up office space in the second floor of the clergy house.

RESTORING THE CHURCH WITH
PHYSICAL PLANT CHANGES

The combined parishioners of St. Andrew's Episcopal Church and the fledgling mission of the Episcopal Inner City Church numbered around fifty people. Together they tackled the challenges of repair and restoration of the parish.

In the church building, the undercroft had served as sleeping quarters for the Donati brothers and visiting guests. A long, narrow hall down the middle had small cells on either side with bunk beds for the Donati brothers. Open floor space with mats housed the visitors from downtown Denver streets. After the monastery ended, the undercroft was repurposed for the offices of the two service organizations.

In the clergy house, the monks of the Order of the Holy Family had created small cells for their sleeping quarters on the second floor. The abbot's quarters consisted of a small room next to the front door of the clergy house. In addition, the architectural archway that connected the common room and the dining room of the clergy house had been boarded up during the monastery years.

When the monastery ended in the summer of 1984, the remaining parishioners along with the Episcopal Inner City Church members began the task of restructuring the church building and clergy house.

Partitions were removed. Doors were sanded. Floors were cleaned. Walls were painted. Furniture was replaced. Parts of the electrical system were upgraded. It involved hundreds of hours of volunteer labor.

In the nave, pews were returned from storage. Monastic stalls from the abbey years were removed. Repair and restoration of the nave was undertaken by the next chapter in the story of St. Andrew's history with the arrival of its new vicar, the Rev. Canon Kenneth Near. Ongoing restoration of the physical plant continued for the next two decades.

DECISION TO BECOME A MISSION

On October 19, 1986, the congregation voted to become an urban mission owned and operated by St. John's Episcopal Cathedral. The Episcopal diocese and St. John's Cathedral valued the unique location of St. Andrew's Episcopal Church on the edge of downtown Denver. A dual ministry of outreach to those in need coupled with enrichment opportunities of education, music, and art was envisioned by the dean of St. John's Cathedral, the Very Rev. Donald McPhail.

Another clergy at the cathedral, the Rev. Canon Kenneth Near, indicated, "There is no Episcopal congregation focusing on the new urban population living in and near downtown . . . St. Andrew's has a long tradition of ministry to the poor, and we think a rejuvenated parish can continue that work, and expand it."[7]

The parish was about to enter a new chapter in its history. The Rev. Canon Near from St. John's Cathedral was about to be named the new vicar of the congregation.

7. Mattingly, "Historic Parish."

5

The Rev. Kenneth Near

Vicar of St. Andrew's Episcopal Church
1986–1991

As we walk the way to wholeness,
Sacrifice befits our call,
Knowing not the cost, we promise,
To be faithful to God's call.
ALLELULA
Blest are those who follow You now.

—final verse of the hymn "Jesus Came
Among Us Gently," by the Rev. Kenneth Near,
to honor the first disciple, Andrew

The Rev. Canon Kenneth Mark Near was called by Bishop William Frey to serve as vicar in the mission parish of St. Andrew's Episcopal Church in December 1986. Fr. Near was tasked with rebuilding the tiny congregation and restoring the century-old building. Fr. Near became the first clergy in nearly sixty years to live in a private residence apart from the parish instead of living in the clergy house, built in 1928. He was also the first known clergy with a family of wife and children to serve as the spiritual leader of the parish.

In five short years, the parish restoration gave birth to a historic new direction in ministry that incorporated the gay community. The church building was restored. Worship centered on Anglo-Catholic liturgy with an evolving emphasis on music. Seeds were planted for pastoral and educational ministries that came to full bloom in the brand-new century.

The Rev. Kenneth Near served as vicar and priest developer as the parish was repurposed and restored from 1986 to 1991.

RE-ENVISIONING ST. ANDREW'S FUTURE

Fr. Ken Near first viewed the transitional state of the parish in 1985, prior to his becoming vicar. "During his first visit to the sanctuary he saw both its glory and signs of years of decline."

The Rev. Kenneth Near

"I looked around," Near recalled, "and said to myself, 'My God, what has happened to this place?'"[1]

The sanctuary roof leaked. The plaster walls were crumbling. The floor tiles were cracked or missing. Pews and other furnishings were damaged.

Out of the ruins came inspiration. Fr. Near was currently serving as a canon (priest) at St. John's Cathedral. He remembered a 1985 financial gift to the cathedral of $1,500,000. A natural connection occurred to Fr. Near of matching a need with a generous gift. He proposed that the cathedral make a biblical tithe of 10 percent of the large gift toward support of St. Andrew's parish and become its financial sponsor. The request amounted to $150,000 for St. Andrew's. The proposal was accepted.

Bishop William Frey agreed with the proposal and appointed Fr. Near as vicar of St. Andrew's Episcopal Church in December 1986. This became the fourth time in the parish history that it experienced mission status—with dependence upon external financial support. The difference this time was that the cathedral, rather than the diocese, served as sponsor.

As the new vicar and congregation began their "way to wholeness," a primary focus was the rebuilding of the nave for worship. The cathedral allocated its gift of $150,000 for repairs and restoration of the worship space. In addition, the Women of St. John's Cathedral provided a major grant for sanctuary furnishings.

VOLUNTEER LABOR FOR RESTORATION

Volunteer workers ranged from the professional to the amateur. Professional architect Gary Long "donated his time to design the drawings, develop the specifications, and meet for long hours with Canon Near, senior warden Judith James, and Gordon Appel of the St. John's vestry property committee to choose paint colors and decide various crucial detail. Gary also worked closely with general contractor Warren Shannon, a friend of the parish, to assure quality

1. Mattingly, "St. Andrew's Feasts."

construction for future generations of parishioners."[2] Both architect and contractor donated considerable time to the project.

In addition, both women's and men's groups from the cathedral and St. Andrew's volunteered time, energy, and gifts. "Week by week a dozen or so parishioners gathered on most Saturday mornings,"[3] according to Fr. Near. Work included carpentry, electrical work, painting, and plumbing. Their intense ongoing labor created a bond among the parishioners. In the process, the congregation grew and attracted more and more people who offered gifts to the emerging new space.

Interior gifts from St. John's Women included the pulpit donated by Mrs. Helene Marsh in memory of her husband, the Archdeacon M. Lewis Marsh Jr. The altar rail was also a gift from the St. John's Women.

Pulpit, altar rail, shelves for candles, and tabernacle were designed and carved by local craftsman Tom Hinz.

Parishioner Martha Bollenbacher designed needlepoint kneeling cushions for the altar rail. An additional sixteen parishioners worked with Martha to create the thirteen needlepoint cushions.

Lighting fixtures on walls and ceiling were a gift from the Newell Sargent Foundation.

Longtime cathedral member Don Allen created a new copper cover and bowl for the historic baptismal font as well as Stations of the Cross reproduced in bronze from original molds designed by Marion Buchan. Don also designed and made a bronze saltire cross with St. Andrew which was originally placed on the face of the high altar. Later it was relocated to the wall next to the organ console.

A wooden pedestal for the statue of Marion Buchan's *Byzantine Madonna* was a gift from McGregor Folsom.

The landscaping design for the parish grounds was created and donated by Richard Marshall of St. John's Cathedral. Men of the cathedral donated their time and labor for the implementation of the

2. James, "Re-Dedication," 4.

3. Ken Near, interview, January 12, 2020.

design. In addition, Fr. Near and parishioner Ron Sellers "labored for many hours, digging and planting, to bring the plan to fruition."[4]

New pews were made possible by parishioners who raised funds with musical soirees along with cathedral support.

In addition, members of both the St. Andrew's parish and St. John's Cathedral "worked to spruce up the exterior and the interior of the Parish House"—formerly the clergy house.[5]

CELEBRATING THE RESTORATION

The feast day of St. Andrew on November 30, 1988 marked the culmination of long days, weeks, and months of restoring the main floor and grounds of St. Andrew's Episcopal Church. The church was rededicated that evening in a memorable and festive celebration.

The nave was repaired, repainted, and refurnished in 1988.

4. James, "Re-Dedication," 5.
5. James, "Re-Dedication," 5.

Suffragan Bishop of Colorado the Rt. Rev. William Wolfram presided. Also participating was the dean of St. John's Cathedral, the Very Rev. Donald McPhail, along with St. Andrew's vicar, the Rev. Canon Kenneth Near.

The preacher was the Rt. Rev. Henry Hill of the Anglican Church of Canada. He was cochair of the Anglican/Eastern Orthodox dialogue. He was the first Anglican bishop since the Reformation to live and pray with Roman Catholic Benedictine monks. On a personal level, "Canon Near credits Bishop Hill with being a key influence on his own spirituality and call to the priesthood." Fr. Near further described Bishop Hill as "a man of prayer, a man of great intellect, and a man of compassion."[6]

Following the joyful rededication service at St. Andrew's, a grand dinner feast was held at the cathedral. A double-decker shuttle bus provided transportation to and from the rededication service.

In contrast to the formal and distinguished celebration, the last-minute preparations were described in the *Rocky Mountain News* from December 3, 1988. "Electricians were rushing to finish their work, hanging beautiful handmade iron light fixtures and pulling down the last of the scaffolds used by volunteer and professional repair crews." Fr. Near explained that "We ran the workmen out the door while other people were mopping up the plaster powder off the floor . . . Then we had to find a way to get 200-plus people in here . . . Finally, people were able to center themselves and worship—miraculously. It was an amazing scene."[7]

THE COLUMBARIUM

Among the initial changes in the church building and traditions of the congregation was the columbarium.

The earliest records of a columbarium date back to January 17, 1978. According to the parish register of 1932–2000, the first inurnment of ashes in a parish columbarium was for John David

6. "Bishop Hill," 2.
7. Mattingly, "St. Andrew's Feasts."

Titus on the 1978 date. He was born in 1921 and raised in the St. Andrew's parish when Fr. Neil Stanley was rector. He died of a fall on the ice that fractured his skull. At the time of Mr. Titus' death, Fr. Jon Marr Stark was the rector of the parish. He was also the abbot of the Order of the Holy Family.

Fr. Jon made use of the historic baptismal font base as the columbarium. Several other persons' ashes were inurned in the baptismal font columbarium in 1979 and 1981.

After Fr. Near became vicar, the columbarium was shifted from the baptismal font to the high altar in the chancel. The change was part of the restoration of the nave.

Fr. Near celebrates the Eucharist from the newly positioned altar.

Fr. Near describes the process of change. ". . . the high altar was firmly attached to the wall and still placed under the reredos. If the high altar was used, this meant that the priest would have his/her back to the congregation during the consecration prayer. When we restored the sanctuary in the eighties, we detached the high altar and moved it several feet toward the congregation. We also had to reinforce the flooring underneath in order to bear the weight of the altar. We removed the cremated remains from the baptismal font base and placed them into the altar."[8] The first three inurnments of ashes during Fr. Near's ministry were parishioners who died of AIDS: Ted Brown, Kenny Waters, and Christopher Parker.

AIDS CRISIS AND ITS IMPACT

In the early days of Fr. Near's ministry at St. Andrew's, a few parishioners from St. John's Cathedral joined Fr. Near's work of the inner-city parish on Glenarm Place. One of those cathedral transplants was Eleanor Brown.

Fr. Near describes the situation:

> Her beloved son, Ted, was critically ill with AIDS and I visited Ted regularly. Several of his friends from the Curtis Park neighborhood became interested in the parish. These included Bob Davis and Ron Sellers. Bob and Ron, along with Billy Oldham, Larry Ballesteros, Chris Van Someren, Chris Parker, the Lemon Family and several others . . . did heroic multiple duties. They looked after their friends with HIV, showed up every Saturday to work on the church restoration, and attended mass on Sundays. They also expressed interest and affection for Anglo-Catholic liturgy. This liturgy became the standard whether our small band worshipped in the Parish House or in the Church.

We watched helplessly as Kenny Waters and Chris Parker slowly deteriorated before our eyes as we labored in love together. I buried Kenny Waters, Chris Parker, and Ted Brown from St. Andrew's. [Note: These three gentlemen were the first whose ashes were inurned in the high altar columbarium.]

In addition, our small parish community had numerous friends who were seriously ill with HIV and many of them died in the 1980s. They were, in reality, part of our "extended community." Yes, parishioners looked after one another but they also were connected to those who had little sense of affiliation to a mainline church.

8. Ken Near, interview, July 19, 2018.

Because I was known outside the traditional boundaries of parish life, I was frequently asked to preside or say a word of comfort at funerals in private homes or at graveyard committals. Some of these were bikers (members of gangs, etc.) and did not want their loved ones listed in a church registry. I became a "chaplain" as it were for the marginalized. I also did a few "traditional" funerals at the cathedral for people with HIV that are not listed at St. Andrew's Church. When I said I did seventeen funerals one summer, I was not exaggerating. However, many are not listed in the parish registry. Nevertheless, I felt deeply connected to them.[9]

His pastoral work during the intense AIDS crisis led Fr. Near to write poetry about his pastoral experiences. He also wrote a prose account of the context of his poem concerning parishioner Kenny Waters.

The poem "a priest to the temple" was composed October 8, 1999. It concerns a haunting pastoral experience with Kenny Waters. "My phone rang in the middle of the night from a nurse's station at Denver General Hospital. The nurse told me that Kenny was asking for me and she urged me to come as he was not doing well. These were his last days after a long battle with HIV. I checked my pyx (a small, beautifully silver vessel that clergy use to transport the sacrament to the sick) and it was empty. So, I had to first stop at St. Andrew's on my way to hospital. The 'temple' in the poem was St. Andrew's Church about midnight between a Sunday and a Monday It was a powerful pastoral moment. His requiem was celebrated shortly thereafter."[10]

A PRIEST TO THE TEMPLE
the phone jarred the darkness
the priest stirred
then made his way
to the temple

the candlelit tabernacle
seen through smoke

9. Ken Near, interview, July 11, 2018.
10. Ken Near, interview, February 6, 2018.

twelve hours old
glowed warmly in the now cold church

true food
was retrieved and brought
to hospital
where our deepest fears are foreshadowed
in the darkness of hallways late at night

a frightened young man
clad in a grotesque gown—very much alone
took his feeble damp hand-—and held it out
hungering for a touch
that told him he mattered

deeply sad eyes revealed his desolation
and unspeakable loneliness

kissed—caressed
hugged—held
anointed—fed
truly loved
he was comforted—for now[11]

Two Denver Episcopal parishes, St. Barnabas and St. Andrew's, became havens for AIDS patients and gay persons during the 1980s and into the 1990s. The natural process of parishioners following their instincts and joining Fr. Near's ministry at St. Andrew's—coupled with their bringing along their friends—culminated in a tiny congregation becoming an open and affirming congregation over time. The organic growth of gay-straight diversity resulted from the compassionate ministry of priest and parish. It was not the result of discernment and decision prompted by ecclesiastical process.

Parishioner Judith James also pointed out that "non-parishioners who attended the many St. Andrew's funerals for persons who died of AIDS sometimes returned to the parish for worship and ended up as participants in parish life."[12]

11. Ken Near, interview, February 6, 2018.
12. Judith James, interview, August 17, 2016.

Both worship and outreach ministries reflected the parish core values. In September 1991, on the feast day of St. Luke, the parish offered a healing service for persons with HIV-AIDS. As the decade of the 1990s unfolded, St. Andrew's became instrumental in the formation of Bethany House, an apartment complex that provided apartments for persons who were dying of AIDS.

CONGREGATIONAL GROWTH

In 1986 when Fr. Near first began his ministry at St. Andrew's, very few parishioners were present. "Because we were so small, everything was done together. All decisions and actions were done as a group,"[13] according to parishioner Judith James.

"For the first few months that I served," says Fr. Near, "the parish consisted of Brother Richard Stockton, Tony Good (both from the Order of the Holy Family), Judith James, and Frank Conner. Tom Titus and Roy Butler were not active when I arrived, but after contacting them, they soon returned."[14]

From this tiny seedling of a parish, the next five years developed like a tree. As Fr. Near explains, "Between my time, the generosity of the cathedral and numerous saintly volunteers, and inspirational community spirit, the congregation rallied and mushroomed in size."[15]

Sunday worship began with five or six and steadily increased, according to the parish register, into the forties, fifties, sixties and beyond. All major liturgical events such as Christmas and Easter completely filled all eighty-eight pews and additional seating.

As the congregation grew, so grew the church ministries. At the end of Fr. Near's second year, a parish newsletter began. Fr. Near named it *Saint Andrew's Network* with the masthead depicting the first disciple's fishing net. The monthly publication, edited by Judith James, continued for the next decade. Because of the newsy little

---

13. Judith James, interview, August 17, 2016.
14. Ken Near, interview, July 11, 2018.
15. Ken Near, interview, July 11, 2018.

paper, much of the congregational growth and development during the late 1980s and 1990s was recorded.

RENEWAL OF ANGLO-CATHOLIC LITURGY

Fr. Near was an enthusiastic supporter of the Anglo-Catholic liturgy, which was first introduced to St. Andrew's by the Rev. Neil Stanley (1920–1942.) Evening prayer was instituted early on in Fr. Near's ministry. Initially it was offered daily.

As a trained musician, Fr. Near also valued music in worship. He sang and directed the choir in the beginning of his ministry at St. Andrew's. However, other trained musicians kept turning up. One of the earliest was Charlotte Dupree, who played the piano for worship in the common room of the Parish House, then the organ in the newly refurbished sanctuary. As she was leaving, Charles van Gunten came on board. Fr. Near was particularly struck by van Gunten's improvisation and his "polish as an accompanist in hymn singing."[16]

Following van Gunten (who went on to become a physician), Joe Griffiths served as organist and choirmaster. Joe also served as parish administrator in the church office and did restoration work of several wooden sculptures in the nave. The earliest church musicians of this era were volunteers since financial sources were not available for musician salaries.

In celebration of St. Andrew's feast day, a special worship service was held on the eve of St. Andrew's, November 29, 1987. Fr. Near wrote the processional hymn for the occasion.

JESUS CAME AMONG US GENTLY
Hymn text: the Reverend Canon Kenneth M. Near
Hymn tune: Saint Osmond by Healey Willan

Jesus came among us gently,
Manifesting love divine.
And he grew to full adulthood,
Showing us God's love so kind.

16. Ken Near, interview, July 11, 2018.

ALLELUIA
Blest are You for sharing Your love.

As they walked along the seashore,
Jesus called some fishermen.
Andrew was the first to follow,
Bringing Peter to God then.
ALLELUIA
Blest were those who followed God's call.

Andrew was the first to follow,
Is today recalled with love.
Pain and suffering he did carry,
To a place with God above.
ALLELUIA
Blest was he who followed you, Lord.

As we walk our way to wholeness,
Sacrifice befits our call.
Knowing not the cost, we promise
To be faithful to God's call.
ALLELUIA
Blest are those who follow You now.[17]

PARISH DEVELOPMENT TAKES OFF

After three years of Fr. Near's ministry, the fragility of the parish had become increasingly steadied. Clear signs of emerging health were reflected in the pledges for the 1990 calendar year. "Pledge income was more than 40 percent above the budget expectation figure."[18]

The parish was paying for its own operating and occupancy costs. St. John's Cathedral was paying for the vicar's salary, housing, and benefits. Special gifts outside the budget covered renovation of the undercroft, the bronzing of the Stations of the Cross, materials for the needlepoint kneelers, and bedding plants.

17. Ken Near, interview, February 6, 2018.
18. James, "New Dean's Committee," 1.

The dean's committee, which served as a vestry, was led by Betty Luce as senior warden and Ron Sellers as junior warden. Five parish committees spearheaded the developing ministries: service, worship, evangelism, education, and pastoral care.

Further expansion of ministry in early 1990 included the addition of a priest associate, the Rev. William E. Pounds. The position was non-stipendiary. Fr. Pounds was employed at Presbyterian-St. Luke's Hospital as Director of Pastoral Care and Education. He became closely associated with Fr. Ken Near and St. Andrew's during the restoration of the parish.

MINISTRIES BEGIN TO FORM

In August 1989, the parish newsletter, *Saint Andrew's Network*, heralded a significant grant for a new ministry.

"Father Ken Near recently announced that St. Andrew's has been awarded a grant by the United Thank Offering of the Episcopal Church. The $11,625 grant will provide initial funding for the St. Andrew's Center for Racial and Ethnic Understanding.

"The grant will provide fifteen months of funding to employ a part-time staff person and promote the Center's activities and program. The Center's office will be located in St. Andrew's Parish House. A Committee chaired by Fr. Near is being formed to provide oversight for the project."[19]

AFTER-SCHOOL TUTORIAL PROGRAM

The following year, this grant-funded program began to take shape. Parishioner Dan James served as the part-time coordinator. College student interns from the Auraria campus were slated to participate along with parish adults from St. Andrew's.

The after-school program targeted neighborhood elementary students. Students were given a light meal followed by help with homework or age-appropriate educational activity.

19. James, "UTO Grant," 1.

Parishioner Martha Bollenbacher remembers that "most of the students were African Americans. Roughly ten students participated along with four or five tutors. These sessions were offered several times each week."[20] Occasionally Martha drove students to their homes after the tutoring.

CHRISTIAN EDUCATION

Both a children's Sunday school and adult education program came into being. The children met on Sunday mornings during the Solemn Eucharist service. Adults gathered on Monday evenings for evening prayer, Eucharist, dinner, and education. The evening provided two offerings: a parishioner Bible study and a college group from the Auraria campus and Regis College. The collegiate group was led by Fr. Near and seminarian David Hutchingson-Tipton.

FROM PLASTER DUST TO NEW LIFE

As the new decade of the 1990s unfolded, the revived parish of St. Andrew's Episcopal Church took on new life. In addition to Anglo-Catholic worship and developing ministries of the congregation, familiar signs of vibrancy reflected its revival.

Fundraisers included the sale of Christmas cards depicting heritage embroideries from former vestments. The holiday cards were sold at the Denver Art Museum and the gift shop at St. John's Cathedral. Other fundraisers included musical variety shows with a cast of notables. The most comprehensive fundraiser involved weekly Lenten lunches. Organist Joe Griffiths prepared soup. Parishioners donated salads and desserts. Luncheon guests included downtown folks, neighbors, and cathedral members. In one year, $2,500 was raised during the Lenten season of lunches.

A ministry fair in September 1990 offered a meet-and-greet of newly formed committees of hospitality, outreach, money, education, worship, arts and architecture, recreation, and kitchen. Also

20. Bollenbacher, Martha interview, February 2, 2017.

included were representatives of acolytes, altar guild, choir, and parish newsletter.

Outreach ministries of local service groups and wider church ministries connected the parish to a network of compassionate care. The parish newsletter offered detailed opportunities of giving or service to Habitat for Humanity, CROP Walkathon, and Denver organizations of the Central Denver Community Service and the Episcopal Pastoral Center.

Social events, particularly in the summer, included parish picnics, white-water rafting, and the Shakespeare festival in Boulder, Colorado. Invitations to summertime diocesan conferences were also extended through the parish newsletter.

HERITAGE ARTWORK

Earlier acquisitions of parish art had deteriorated over time. Several legacy sculptures were preserved during this restoration chapter of the parish.

One of the oldest carvings was the *Byzantine Madonna* made by Marion Buchan during the ministry of the Rev. Neil Stanley (1920–1942.) During Fr. Near's ministry, the statue was cleaned up and restored by Don Allen in 1988.

A wooden sculpture of St. Andrew was acquired during Fr. Justin Van Lopik's ministry (1954–1969.) The sculpture was donated by Verna Schneider in memory of her mother. In 1989, organist Joe Griffith removed old paint and varnish and restored the original wood artwork.

Following the closure of St. Mark's Episcopal Church at Twelfth and Lincoln in downtown Denver, the diocese distributed furnishings from St. Mark's to various mission congregations. St. Andrew's parish was given a brass lectern featuring an eagle with the feet of a lion. St. Andrew's also received a carved wooden credence table plus an ample supply of Eucharistic linens.

CONTINUING GIFTS

Parishioners and friends continued to offer gifts for the restored building and grounds. Included was an altar cross with a wooden base and bronze figure of Christ donated by Ron Sellers and Bob Davis. It was given in 1989 in memory of Bob's mother, Gertrude Davis.

Oak choir chairs were donated by Ed and Nancy Pierson in 1989.

An oak handrail on either side of the steps leading to the chancel was designed and made by artist Tom Hinz in 1991.

Outside the church building, several gifts were given by parishioners. Roy Butler donated a tree, which was planted in the right-of-way in front of the church in 1989. It was in memory of Jessie Kent.

A large, ornamental wrought iron sign with moveable lettering and lighted signboard was also donated in 1989. Donors were Bob Davis, Ron Sellers, and Sharon Leslie. The gift was in memory of Ron Sellers's parents—Dorothy and Marion Sellers.

The undercroft was considerably remodeled with a large bequest from the estate of Tony Good in addition to other special gifts. By late fall of 1990, the undercroft had been transformed into a parish hall. It included a kitchen, classroom space, choir rehearsal room, a vesting area, and treasurer's office.

THE NEAR FAMILY

Fr. Near's wife Karen was one of the seventeen needlepointers who worked for long months creating the thirteen kneeler cushions for placement in front of the chancel railing in the nave. Each cushion depicted the symbol of one of the twelve disciples. The thirteenth cushion represented Mathias, who became a disciple after Judas' departure. Karen was also a teacher in the children's Sunday school as well as a public school teacher in Denver.

In September 1989, Martin Near (age ten) was invited to attend the St. Thomas Choir School in New York City. The Choir School is a world-class four-year music program for boys in the fifth through eighth grades. Martin had been a member of the St.

John's Cathedral choir for two years. His clear soprano voice and superior musical aptitude led to his auspicious invitation.

"Martin's farewell . . . was bittersweet. Martin loves and excels at music and there was great excitement and joy over this unique opportunity for excellent musical training. However, the joy was touched with sadness for the Near family . . . who will miss Martin."[21]

Younger sister Lydia Near was featured in the "Personality Profile" of the parish newsletter of February–March 1990. On the heels of her brother Martin's move to New York City to participate in the St. Thomas Choir School, she acknowledged that "it's lonely being a newly single child, but the good side is that her parents take her out to dinner more often."[22]

FR. NEAR MOVES TO A NEW POSITION

Essentially five years after becoming vicar of St. Andrew's, Fr. Near was called to a new position in Englewood, New Jersey. He became rector of St. Paul's Episcopal Church in Englewood in November 1991.

"It was important to us to get our family back together on a more permanent basis," Fr. Near said, "and I saw this as a great opportunity to take the next step in my career. The hardest thing for us to do is leave our friends at St. Andrew's. Our relationships with the people here have been stimulating, loving and supportive—something we will miss terribly as we go on to our new life."[23]

LEGACY OF FR. NEAR

An extraordinary five years of ministries by Fr. Near steered the remnant community—the "household of St. Andrew"—from the brink of nonexistence to a vibrant and life-affirming parish. Both the building and the congregation grew stronger together. As the

21. James, "Martin Near," 2.
22. Steele, "Personality Profiles," 5.
23. Christensen, "Father Near," 1.

worship space was restored, people were drawn into the restoration work from St. John's Cathedral as well as friends and neighbors.

Along the way, gay citizens of the city became involved in the engaging work, the worship of the parish, and in outreach beyond the walls. Like a garden in happy soil, the little parish on the edge of downtown began blooming with diversity of gay and straight parishioners. Just in time for the emerging AIDS crisis.

Pastoral care for those dying, plus many funerals, and a searing sense of loss led to hard thinking about housing solutions for AIDS patients whose resources were diminished. Caring for youngsters of the neighborhood prompted tutoring services by parishioners. Embedded in the DNA of the newly restored parish was a commitment to serve those not being served.

Step by step, the ravages of time were stripped away. A restored community of faith emerged into a fresh, new form. New seeds were planted for further life-giving ministries "in their own backyard" in the immediate years ahead.

6

The Rev. Connie Delzell

Rector of St. Andrew's Episcopal Church
1991–2007

Jesus said, "Let the little children come to me, and do not stop
them; for it is to such as these that the kingdom of heaven
belongs."

—Matthew 9:14, illustrated in the central panel of the
reredos above the altar at St. Andrew's Episcopal Church

The year 1991 marked the first time a woman served as the clerical leader of the parish. The Rev. Constance Delzell served under
three titles in her sixteen years at St. Andrews: first as interim vicar,
then vicar, and finally as rector. Her signature vision centered on
neighborhood children and their education, which culminated in
the establishment of St. Elizabeth's School in Denver. Other seminal ministries of the Rev. Delzell included the founding of Bethany
House for persons dying of AIDS, direct mentoring of women
clergy, implementing exemplary music in worship, and leading the
little church from mission status to parish status. Along the way,

the church building was restored from a major fire, then followed by expansion and remodeling of the sanctuary several years later.

BIOGRAPHICAL BACKGROUND

Constance K. Clawson born December 31, 1942, Carmi, Illinois

Father Darrell B. Clawson, chemical engineer

Mother Gertrude Gorman Clawson, Millsaps College administrator, Jackson, Mississippi, and housewife

Sister Darrelyn Clawson Sanders born 1947

Brother Gary Dennis Clawson, 1949–2001

Constance K. Clawson married David W. Delzell February 23, 1962; David Delzell born October 25, 1938, Enid, Oklahoma, mortage banker

Daughter Heather Delzell, married to Shane McKay, sons Garrett and Jonathan McKay

Formative influences: lifelong Episcopalian, 1928 *Book of Common Prayer*, 1960s civil rights movement, daughter's struggles with dyslexia, brother's pain and discrimination as a gay person

EDUCATION AND ORDINATION

BA in religious studies, magna cum laude, 1977, University of Colorado, Boulder

Clinical Pastoral Education, June–September 1980, Boulder Community Hospital

MAR, with distinction, 1981, Iliff School of Theology, Denver

Certificate in Anglican Studies, 1981–1983, Seabury–Western Theological Seminary, Evanston, Illinois

Pastoral Counseling Supervision, 1981–1984, Iliff School of Theology, Denver

Ordination as a deacon, June 4, 1983, Denver

Ordination as a priest, December 6, 1983, Denver (first woman to complete entire ordination process in the diocese of Colorado)

Continuing Education:
Pastoral Care and Congregational Development

Workshop/training as Evangelism Consultant, 1984, Burlingame, California

Workshop on Congregational Development, 1986, Denver, Colorado

Workshop on Stewardship, 1988, Nashota House, Wisconsin

Postgraduate work in Marriage and Family Counseling, 1990–1992, Colorado Institute for Marriage and Family, Denver

Postgraduate studies in Care and Consultation of Congregations, 2004, Iliff School of Theology, Denver

Workshop "Start Up! Start Over!," 2005, Office for Parish Development, Episcopal Church, USA

CLERGY POSITIONS

Associate Rector, 1982–1985, St. John's Episcopal Church, Boulder

Founding Vicar, 1983–1990, St. Mary Magdalene Church, Boulder

Canon Pastor, Episcopal Diocese of Colorado, 1990–1991

Canon Missioner, St. John's Cathedral, 1992–2000, Denver; simultaneously, Vicar, St. Andrew's Episcopal Church, 1991–2000

JOINING THE RESTORATION PROCESS

Mother Connie, at age forty-nine, was called by Bishop Jerry Winterrowd to continue the buildup of the parish life and ministries at St. Andrew's Episcopal Church. Following the closing of the St. Andrew's Abbey and its monastic life in 1984, initial parish restoration was spearheaded by the Rev. Kenneth Near from 1986 to 1991. Fr. Near made significant headway in rebuilding the worship space and restarting parish life. Seedling ministries were planted during the years of his work and then continued and expanded by Mother Connie.

Both Fr. Ken Near and Mother Connie specialized in congregational development. However, they had distinctly different gifts and offered different skills to the redevelopment of the parish. Their work dovetailed effectively in restoring the congregational life and work of St. Andrew's Episcopal Church.

INITIATING A NEW CHAPTER

In December 1991, Mother Connie was welcomed to St. Andrew's Episcopal Church as interim vicar. By July 1992 she was named vicar. Eight years later, in 2000, Mother Connie became rector when the parish celebrated its transition from mission status to parish status—from financial dependence upon St. John's Cathedral to financial independence.

Mother Connie's leadership steered the congregation into financial independence by increasing membership, strengthening stewardship, expanding ministries, and advancing the musical excellence of the liturgy. Worship attendance doubled from the sixties in 1991 to well over one hundred by the new century. Annual stewardship efforts exceeded their financial goals. Ministries of education and well-being blossomed both inside and outside the parish.

In 1995, new musical leadership was established that led to musical prominence for St. Andrew's Anglo-Catholic worship. Choirmaster Tim Krueger and organist Richard Robertson were hired. The parish offered Tim Krueger office space for his St. Martin's Chamber Choir. Thus began a quarter-century of choral music at St. Andrew's that has distinguished it ever since.

SUPPORTING WOMEN IN MINISTRY

Mother Connie was the first woman to complete the ordination process within the Episcopal Diocese of Colorado in 1983. As a pioneer of ecclesiastical equality, she mentored other women who followed in her footsteps. During her sixteen-year ministry at St. Andrews Episcopal Church, five women served the parish as deacons or curates on their way to becoming priests within the diocese.

During the 1990s, the trailblazing women included Marilyn Schneider, Felicia Smith Graybeal, Rebecca Ferrell Nickel, Michelle Quinn-Miscall, and Nancee Martin-Coffey.

In 1995, besides initiating new musical leadership, Mother Connie invited the Rev. Sally Brown to serve as deacon. Deacon Sally continued to serve St. Andrew's for the next fourteen years. An extraordinary partnership developed between the two women. Sharing the preaching tasks was a hallmark of their collaboration.

The Rev. Sally Brown (left) with Bishop Winterrowd and the Rev. Connie Delzell, 2000

Deacon Sally recounted a particular Sunday morning when it was time for the sermon. "Rev. Connie turned to me and mentioned it was time for me to move to the pulpit for the sermon. I reminded her that it was her turn to give the sermon that day. Although totally forgetting that it was her turn, Rev. Connie walked to the pulpit and gave an extemporaneous and splendid sermon."[1]

In describing the differences in their preaching styles, Deacon Sally characterized her own sermons as based on "street images." She characterized Mother Connie's sermons as reflecting "orthodox understandings from a distinctly Anglican perspective." Deacon Sally continued. "I would shake it up and Rev. Connie would put it back together."[2]

In addition to shared preaching, the two women shared teaching tasks. Both priest and deacon jointly taught the catechumenate class, preparing a total of some one hundred parishioners to serve as a core of leadership among the laity. Another coteaching project was the Education for Ministry program. An ambitious three-year program, it covered Scripture, church history, and theology—a curriculum designed by an Episcopal seminary.

Embracing her longtime engagement with those most vulnerable and neglected, Deacon Sally led the congregation to an awareness of and contribution to various outreach ministries. She "led the congregation out the door," in her words, to be advocates and participants in a range of mission activities. Deacon Sally was a staunch supporter of the immediate neighborhood initiatives in education. She actively supported the Bethany House project. Deacon Sally also introduced the parish to both local and global missions. She saw herself as the "pusher" and the parishioners as the "doers."[3]

In contrast to her visible leadership, Deacon Sally also embodied quiet and unassuming ministry that was largely invisible to the public. She intentionally removed her clerical collar in order to foster trust building when she engaged with homeless neighbors who were put off by clerical attire. According to Deacon Sally, "My real passion is to bring a quiet presence to those we serve."

1. Sally Brown, interview, July 24, 2016.
2. Sally Brown, interview, July 24, 2016.
3. Sally Brown, interview, July 24, 2016.

She referred to her neighborly visits as "a Sacrament of the Present Moment" to underscore her ministry of simply being present with others.[4] Among her comrades in the parish rose garden were Gus and Nancy, whom she joined in the evenings on occasion. A quiet bond marked their interaction.

A MEDITATION GARDEN

Also growing into life in the mid-1990s was a meditation garden on the west side of the church building. Mother Connie imagined a rarely used space behind the church and Parish House as a garden of contemplation within the protection of trees and a stalwart wall.

Between 1994 and 1995, memorial funding and gifts were provided from various parishioners and friends. The total cost was $13,000. Major memorial gifts came from a financial bequest of the Rev. Emmett Jones and a memorial fund for Charlotte Rice Butler. A bronze memorial plaque on the garden gate names the Rev. Jones and Mrs. Butler as the persons honored by the meditation garden.

Emmett Jones grew up in the clergy house when Fr. Stanley was rector (1920–1942). Jones' mother was Fr. Stanley's housekeeper. Apparently the environment was influential. Emmett Jones became a priest and served as a curate for Fr. Stanley in 1935. During the Rev. Jones's lifetime of ministry, he served as a chaplain in the armed forces. In his later years, he bequeathed Exxon stock to St. Andrew's. It was held in trust by St. John's Cathedral until 1995, when it was designated for the meditation garden in his memory.

The other person memorialized by the meditation garden is *Charlotte Rice Butler*. She grew up in the neighborhood of St. Andrew's Episcopal Church and was confirmed as a member of St. Andrew's in 1928 during Fr. Stanley's ministry as rector. Her husband, Tom Butler, a member of St. John's Cathedral, contributed major support to the garden in her memory.

Architect Gary Long designed the west wall gratis as a gift for the parish. The six-foot wall separated the parish from the alley and gave privacy to the garden. Architect Long designed red brick piers

4. Brown, interview, July 24, 2016.

to match the red brick of the church buildings. They were placed eight feet apart with the wall area between piers built of concrete blocks covered with stucco.

Then the landscaping began under the direction of a parish Arts and Architecture Committee. It was chaired by Martha Bollenbacher. The grassy lawn was complimented by low-maintenance shrubs and perennial plants. Aspen trees were planted along the wall and the back of the church. Completing the landscape were ornamental wooden screens next to the church building and Parish House.

A marble altar and historic stone baptismal font were a focal point of the garden. Behind the altar, a wrought iron cross was installed on the garden wall. Along the wall, the fourteen Stations of the Cross were represented by roman numerals made of wrought iron. Even the wrought iron entrance gate from the parking lot matched the artistic design. Stone benches provided seating.

Mother Connie Delzell celebrates the Eucharist in the newly formed meditation garden, ca. 1996.

On October 1, 1995, the meditation garden was dedicated. It became a special haven for worship and occasional baptism as well as social events. And in between, the garden served its intended purpose of quiet retreat.

SEEDS GROW INTO NEW MINISTRIES—
BETHANY HOUSE

The AIDS crisis emerged during Fr. Ken Near's ministry at St. Andrew's from 1986 to 1991. Fr. Near served as a pastor to may AIDS patients both inside and outside of the church. He officiated at numerous funerals of persons who died of AIDS. In one summer the count was seventeen. The tiny congregation grew into a church family of both gay and straight parishioners.

EARLY EFFORTS TO PROVIDE HOUSING

In the early 1990s, the small St. Andrew's congregation became increasingly concerned about housing needs for AIDS patients who were dying. Parishioners Bob Davis and Ron Sellers were passionate to provide housing for persons with AIDS who had lost their incomes and were unable to provide for themselves.

Parishioners Ron Sellers (left) and Bob Davis initiated the ministry of
housing for persons with AIDS, resulting in Bethany House.

Joining Bob Davis and Ron Sellers were parishioners Betty Luce, Don Romberger, and attorney Sandy Lough. They formed a board of directors. These leaders along with various advisors worked long and hard over several years. They hammered out overall vision and details of execution. They also spearheaded an intensive fundraising effort.

FUNDING

Initial fundraising came from substantial efforts by the congregation. *St. Andrew's Soiree* was an elaborate annual variety show which featured Cleo Parker Robinson children's dance classes, St. Martin's Chamber Choir, jazz singers, and canons (clergy) of St. John's Cathedral, among others. An extensive annual plant sale took place at St. Andrew's and St. John's Cathedral.

A growing consortium of partners provided additional funding. In addition, the wider Episcopal Church offered support through its diocesan conventions and women's conventions, as well as parish presentations supporting Bethany House and the ongoing AIDS battle. The emerging idea of a haven for persons dying of AIDS was promoted by partnerships with the Colorado AIDS Project and AIDS Walk.

These community partners were effective in raising the profile of Bethany House in the Episcopal diocese and larger community. By the mid-1990s, funding came together from 1) a grant from the Oakes Home Trust (an Episcopal foundation), 2) an HUD grant, and 3) a large anonymous donation from a parishioner at St. John's Cathedral. Combined with the congregational fundraisers, these multiple funds enabled a search for a suitable building.

LOCATION AND MINISTRY ESTABLISHED

In 1995, an apartment building was purchased at 1505 East Sixteenth Avenue. The forty-eight apartment units were refurbished with volunteer labor. Half the apartments were made available at low rates to persons dying of AIDS. Another half of the apartments were made available to tenants paying market rent to cover the operating expenses of the building. The three-story building became officially known as Bethany House.

Bethany House was an apartment house at 1505 East Sixteenth Avenue for
persons who were dying of AIDS, 1996–2001.

ONGOING OPERATION OF THE NEW MINISTRY

Bethany House was incorporated as a Colorado nonprofit corporation and received 501(c)(3) status from the Internal Revenue
Service.

Medical research to find a cure for AIDS was proceeding at
a rapid pace in the 1990s. The transmission of the AIDS virus was
spreading widely as a result of the sharing of needles among IV
drug users. So the population of AIDS patients expanded from the
gay community to the larger community.

By the time Bethany House opened in 1996, the first drugs to
prolong the life of AIDS patients became available. It was clear that
the affected population was going to be considerably different from
what the Bethany House founders had envisioned. AIDS patients
would need housing for longer periods of time and case management would be needed to manage complex medications and drug
abuse.

Community rooms and recreational facilities for residents were provided at Bethany House. Onsite management and supportive services became essential. A network of individuals, churches, nonprofit organizations, healthcare providers, and government agencies offered a cafeteria of support services.

St. Andrew's Episcopal Church donated $100 per month for the support of the new ministry. In addition, the church provided office space for Bethany House. In 1995, Michael Knudsen (eventual parishioner of St. Andrew's) was hired as administrative assistant to coordinate with the administrator. Sandy Lough was hired as attorney for the project. According to Michael Knudsen, Mother Connie supported and worked directly in the development of the housing project. At the inauguration of the longtime effort, she officiated at a house blessing for Bethany House.[5]

Household starter kits were donated by St. Andrew's parishioners. They consisted of pots, pans, cooking utensils, dishes, glasses, flatware, table linens, sheets and pillowcases.

In addition, parishioners donated time, money, and plants to landscape Bethany House's front property. Annual plant sales continued in financial support of the ministry. Ongoing fundraising continued through the Colorado AIDS Project, such as the annual bike ride for AIDS along with the annual AIDS walk.

SUCCESSFUL OUTCOMES

In 2000, St. Andrew's experimental ministry was acknowledged and affirmed by the national Episcopal Church. It conferred the status of Jubilee Center upon Bethany House. Jubilee Centers are exemplary ministries within the wider Episcopal Church of congregations providing direct services to "the poor and oppressed" and "meeting basic human needs and building a just society."[6]

In addition, the board of Bethany House was approached by a well-established and well-financed AIDS housing provider in another part of the city. Our House had a smaller hospice facility

5. Michael Knudsen, interview, July 5, 2018.
6. Armentrout and Slocum, *Episcopal Dictionary*, 280.

in south Denver. They proposed that Bethany House merge with Our House. Eventually, the Sixteenth Avenue property was sold and Bethany House operations merged into the Our House project.

MORE SEEDLINGS MATURE—
CHILDREN'S EDUCATION

1989

During Fr. Ken Near's ministry, St. Andrew's Episcopal Church received an $11,625 grant from the United Thank Offering of the Episcopal Church. Its purpose was to fund St. Andrew's Center for Racial and Ethnic Understanding.

1990

The grant funded program began to take shape in the form of after-school tutoring of neighborhood children. Parishioner Martha Bollenbacher remembers ten children participated in the program. "Most were young persons of color. Students were given a light meal followed by help with homework or age appropriate educational activity. Sessions were offered several times a week."[7]

CHANGE IN LEADERSHIP BRINGS
A DIFFERENT GARDNER

1991

When Mother Connie came to St. Andrew's, she brought her perspective from her experiences as a parent. During her daughter Heather's growing-up years, Heather struggled in school because of her dyslexia. Through the Delzell family's love of art and music, Heather discovered her gifts as an artist. As she grew in self-confidence with painting, she also navigated her academic subjects with

7. Martha Bollenbacher, interview, February 2, 2017.

more success. Mother Connie considered how she might help other students who struggled to learn.

After arriving at St. Andrew's, Mother Connie had a dream that she felt was a message from God. The dream instructed her to act on her lessons learned from her daughter Heather's experiences and her parental insights regarding students who struggled in school.

NEIGHBORHOODS SURROUNDING ST. ANDREW'S CHURCH

In addition to the existing fledgling tutoring program of the parish and Mother Connie's happy discovery of the arts as a pathway to learning, the immediate neighborhoods around St. Andrew's offered an ideal opportunity for vision to become reality. The Five Points neighborhood and the Cole neighborhood housed school children who shared some of Heather Delzell's challenges. These inner-city students also struggled with academic subjects and lack of self-confidence. Compounding the students' struggles were pervasive poverty and daily challenges in the home environment.

MODEST BEGINNING BECOMES A MAJOR MINISTRY

1992

St. Andrew's after-school tutorial program served ten neighborhood children twice a week at St. Andrew's Episcopal Church. Students ages seven to twelve enjoyed snacks, recreation, and tutoring.

1993

Enthusiastic partners quickly emerged and worked together for expansion of the original ministry. Initial leaders from the wider Episcopal Church included Dean Kiblinger of St. John's Cathedral along with Bishop Winterrowd and the Rev. Dan Hopkins of the diocese becoming partners with parishioners.

The Children's Arts and Learning Center was welcomed into a building owned by St. John's Cathedral at Twenty-First and Stout Streets. Half the building was used by Metro Caring—a provider of food and related services to those in need. The other half was converted from storage space into the new children's center.

Church partners grew to include neighborhood partners with East Village, a housing complex on Park Avenue West—fairly close to St. Andrew's. East Village was home to some five hundred children. Volunteers from both church and East Village prepared the new center's home by cleaning, painting, and installing flooring.

The Children's Arts and Learning Center was inaugurated during the summer session of 1993 with classes in choral music, photography, painting, drawing, and print making. Field trips included excursions to museums, parks, and Rockies baseball games. Experienced artists and musicians donated their time and services as teachers. Parents from East Village provided volunteer help.

Students enthusiastically participated in art activities at the Children's Arts and Learning Center in the 1990s.

The Children's Arts and Learning Center opened the 1993 fall season with 1) classes in fine arts and crafts, 2) intensive one-on-one tutoring in reading and math, and 3) a music program. Volunteer tutors were supervised by teachers from Denver Public Schools. (Arts and music had been recently cut from public schools in Denver.)

The center served students from Crofton-Ebert and Steele Elementary Schools in grades 1–5 who lived in East Village or surrounding area. The center operated each weekday after school from 4:00 to 5:00 pm.

Governance of the center was provided by a board of directors comprised of members of St. Andrew's Episcopal Church and St. John's Cathedral. It operated as an independent nonprofit corporation. Preplanning of the fall program was done in consultation with school principals and community leaders by Mother Connie and the center's director.

During the center's first year, some twenty-five students ages four to ten were enrolled. A student waiting list was created until further volunteer tutors were available.

From the beginning, each student was paired with an adult tutor who worked with them all year. The children benefitted from the undivided attention from a person who they came to know and bond with and trust. The tutoring relationships led to positive outcomes reported by teachers at Crofton-Ebert and Steele Elementary Schools. They reported improvement in reading, self-expression, leadership, and social interaction with more kindness and compassion toward others.

Math students working with their tutor at the Children's Arts and Learning Center in the 1990s.

In addition to volunteer academic tutors, other volunteers worked with the professional artists who taught the art projects. Training for academic tutors was provided throughout the year by teachers from Denver Public Schools. Donations of art supplies and snack items (fruit and baked goods) were continually offered by St. Andrew's members and others in the wider community.

1994

The second summer session was conducted at the Crofton-Ebert Elementary School, serving children living in East Village. The summer program was sponsored by Denver Parks and Recreation. Again, the summer program consisted of weekday art and music classes with one day devoted to field trips.

In June 1994, the Children's Arts and Learning Center received a $20,000 grant from the city and county of Denver. The grant was part of Denver's Safe City Program, designed to prevent crime and violence.

Mother Connie Delzell accepts the Safe City Award from Denver Mayor Wellington Webb, June 1994.

The highly coveted award had 260 applicants. A total of forty-seven applicants actually received a grant from the program. Grant money was used to add paid staff, including a music director for the center.

Staff served from a wide range of professional backgrounds and expertise. They came from Iliff School of Theology (Denver), the University of Denver, a San Francisco theater company, Colorado Children's Chorale, and Cleo Parker Robinson Dance Theatre (Denver).

Expertise among staff included social workers; graduates in African American studies; those with graduate degrees in fine art, special education, art therapy, and music; and a native of Colombia (South America). Heather Delzell served as art director of the children's center.

St. John's Cathedral provided a van to transport children to their homes in the evening after their tutoring and art classes.

1995–1997

The center continued to thrive and expand to include more and more students. By 1996, the ministry changed location to Annunciation School at 3536 Lafayette Street. Students came primarily from Crofton-Ebert, Gilpin, and Mitchell Elementary Schools.

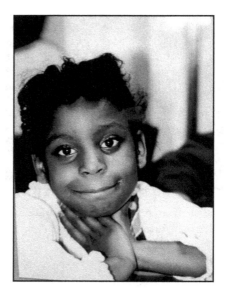

Young students thrived within structured relationships with trained volunteer instructors and well-planned curriculum in the Children's Arts and Learning Center.

Reading and math were academic subjects. Field trip destinations included the Denver Zoo and the Denver Art Museum. End-of-year programs included plays, a Christmas pageant, and children's art exhibits.

1998

The Center continued to grow in its professional expertise and offerings to inner-city children. The 1998 summer session was held at St. John's Cathedral. The 1998 fall session began in a brand-new site: the newly renovated Edison/Wyatt School at Thirty-Sixth and Franklin Streets. Enrollment was ninety students in kindergarten through sixth grade.

Wyatt Edison School was the final location of the Children's Arts and Learning Center from 1998 to ca. 2006.

A MAJOR MINISTRY MATURES AND CELEBRATES

1999

The Children's Center for Arts and Learning entered the year with an annual budget of over $100,000 in grants and private donations. The enrollment was one hundred students.

The summer session was held at St. John's Cathedral with seventy-five students. The summer program was called TRACKS— Teach Reading and Art to Colorado Kids. The summer curriculum focused on the art and culture of China, Ireland, Hawaii, and Alaska and involved dance, vocal music, and art classes.

The fall session opened in the newly renamed Wyatt Edison Charter School. It was the final home of the children's center.

National recognition was conferred on the Children's Arts and Learning Center by the Episcopal Church in the United States. It named the ministry by St. Andrew's Episcopal Church as a Jubilee Center. The designation is bestowed on exemplary ministries that provide direct services to "the poor and oppressed" and which are "meeting basic human needs and building a just society."[8] St. Andrew's ministry to AIDS patients at Bethany House was also named a Jubilee Center in 2000.

In November 2000 a children's choir was organized at the children's center. It was named the Saint Cecilia Singers. Three sponsoring groups were 1) the Children's Center for Arts and Learning, 2) the Episcopal Diocese of Colorado, and 3) St. Andrew's Episcopal Church. The director was Kevin Fletcher, a lead teacher at the Wyatt Edison Charter School. Formerly he directed the Boys and Girls Choir at St. John's Cathedral. John Taylor, St. Andrew's parishioner, was the accompanist.

The group began with thirty-five students who came from throughout the city, primarily from the children's center, and represented a variety of cultural backgrounds from ages eight to fourteen. The Saint Cecilia Singers quickly developed into an accomplished ensemble and gave concerts throughout the city of Denver. Eventually nearly fifty students participated.

In December 2001, the choir was invited to sing at the Washington National cathedral in Washington, DC. The occasion was Colorado Day at the Cathedral and the Saint Cecilia Singers provided a twenty-five-minute choral prelude prior to the 10:30 Sunday morning service.

8. Armentrout and Slocum, *Episcopal Dictionary*, 280.

The Saint Cecelia Singers sang at The Washington National Cathedral, Washington, DC in December 2001.

The Saint Cecilia Singers frequently sang at worship services at St. Andrew's Episcopal Church.

SEEDS BECOME A FULL-GROWN TREE

At the dawn of the twenty-first century, this little parish on the edge of downtown was envisioning yet another significant contribution to the city of Denver.

Ever the visionary, Mother Connie again saw both a problem and a solution. She was disillusioned by the new charter school policies. She also observed that the teaching staff and discipline procedures did not match the needs of the student population. At the same time, she envisioned a more substantial solution to quality education for underserved students. In short, she dreamed of a brand-new Episcopal school in the heart of Capitol Hill.

Parishioner Betty Luce was a key leader in the ministries of Bethany House, the Children's Arts and Learning Center, and St. Elizabeth's School. She continues to the present day as vice president of the board of trustees of the school.

Planning and funding came next. St. Andrew's initial leaders included the Rev. Delzell, the Rev. Richard Valantasis, and Betty Luce. They were soon joined by parishioner Ann Jesse and friend of the parish Dr. Gregory Robbins, of the University of Denver. The group formed a board of directors and immediately began carving out underlying concepts for its dream school. Fundraising followed.

Basic convictions that formed at the very beginning are still the foundation of St. Elizabeth's School at 2350 Gaylord Street. Its multicultural, multiracial makeup was seminal. Its financial format was conceived to underscore the diversity of socioeconomic families. "One third would pay virtually nothing to attend. One third would pay on a sliding scale. One third would essentially pay full tuition."[9] Today the Family Commitment Plan reflects each family's financial commitment, which is equitable to its financial resources.

Experienced with fundraising for Bethany House and the Children's Center for Arts and Learning, the St. Andrew's team quickly launched its search for financial resources. Among the assets acquired was a grant of $300,000 from a Jesuit source.

9. Betty Luce, interview, May 26, 2019

Donations large and small were raised. With amazing tenacity, the congregation pitched in for its continuing and substantive ministries. One of the parishioners declared, "I've invested more money in St. Andrew's ministries than in my own retirement account."

Bishop Robert O'Neill played jazz piano for the St. Elizabeth's School fundraiser, known as the St. Andrew's Soiree.

ST. ELIZABETH'S SCHOOL DEVELOPS

St. Elizabeth's School reflects the pluralism practiced in many private Episcopal schools across the nation. It thrives with students from a range of religious backgrounds (and some with no religious tradition). Instead of indoctrination of beliefs, the school practices core moral values inherent in many world faith traditions (e.g., honoring the dignity of all people, contributing to the common good, and treating others with care and compassion).

Opening in 2007, the school started with kindergarten only. Each year another grade was added (grades 1–5) and finally a middle school was incorporated with grades 6–8. By 2019, enrollment was 155 students.

St. Elizabeth's School, established in 2007, is located at 2350 Gaylord Street in Denver.

The student body is intentionally limited in order to fully serve every student. The student-teacher ratio ranges from 7:1 to 9:1. Every classroom has one teacher and one fully qualified assistant. Exceptional educational opportunity is the goal of St. Elizabeth's School.

A hallmark of the school is its vibrant parent association. The association is a key factor in the formation of a strong sense of community. Their annual auction is a major fundraiser. In 2011, the parent group raised sufficient funding for a new science curriculum for all grade levels. In addition, the director of development coordinates a range of financial revenues.

Like its forerunner, the original Children's Center for Arts and Learning, the new St. Elizabeth's School features rich programs in all the arts. Regular field trips include major art centers along with a variety of other interests.

AN UNWELCOME EVENT LEADS
TO RESTORATION

An enthusiastic Sunday school celebration on October 31, 1999 recreated a Dia de los Muertos—Day of the Dead—altar of remembrance. It was an ambitious display of children's art and candles. Lots of candles.

Parish children prepared candles in front of the altar for the celebration of Dia de los Muertos, October 31, 1999.

Embers from an errant candle slipped unnoticed to the undercroft (basement) floor and beyond in the middle of the night. Flames leapt into the undercroft and upward into the floor of the sanctuary. Observant women at the neighborhood Mercury Cafe at 2199 California Street reported the fire at 1:07 a.m. on Sunday, November 1. No one was injured in the blaze.

Church property, however, was seriously damaged. The community space of the undercroft was destroyed. Above, the sanctuary of the church suffered major damage. A hole was burned into the floor of the south aisle. Smoke extensively damaged ceiling, walls, and artwork. Chandeliers melted. The organ was ruined.

The shocking disaster propelled the congregation to vacate the property. For almost seven months, they worshipped at the Temple Events Center, a former synagogue, at the corner of Sixteenth and Pearl Street.

Mother Connie reported that "the crisis is giving way to God's steadfast providence, the good leadership of so many, and the rallying of the congregation." She continued, "There is not the slightest doubt that God will use this displacement for our good. More blessings will follow from the fire than if the fire had never occurred."[10]

REBUILDING TAKES SHAPE

The financial cost was largely covered by insurance. In total, insurance paid $460,000 of the restoration. However, the portion not covered by insurance was paid by the congregation: $40,000.

Mother Connie appointed an arts and architecture committee to supervise the massive effort of restoration. The group included an architect who was a member of the congregation, Mr. Tee Cowperthwaite. He remembered the details of the original church building. The committee met weekly for nearly seven months.

The University of Denver Conservation Center painstakingly cleaned and restored the reredos above the altar. Created by artist Albert Byron Olson and donated to St. Andrew's in 1931, the five panels had accumulated residue from decades of incense use in addition to smoke damage from the fire. The vibrant colors were restored in a way that gave brilliance to the restored chancel. Additional cleaning and restoration were provided by the Conservation Center for the sculpture of the *Byzantine Madonna*, created by artist Marion Buchan circa 1930.

10. Delzell, "Vicar's Voice," 1.

The 1931 reredos by Albert Byron Olson was cleaned, restored, and put back into place by members of the University of Denver Conservation Center, Spring 2000.

Renovation work included upgrading the heating and electrical systems of the parish. The result provided better lighting for both the sanctuary and undercroft.

One of the costliest replacements was the church organ. A capital campaign of the parish raised over $300,000 for the newly selected Buzard organ. An anonymous donor contributed one third of that amount. Insurance paid for $57,000. The extensive fundraising provided for both the newly built organ and also for long-term maintenance. The organ fundraising and purchase took place in 2001.

On May 24, 2000—over half a year after the fire—the congregation was led back into its stunningly restored Church Home by Bishop Winterrowd. "With a rap of his crozier (shepherd's staff) on the entry door, the Rt. Rev. Jerry Winterrowd proclaimed, 'Let the doors be opened.'"[11]

11. Lyon, "Hopes Restored," 4.

Mother Connie, Deacon Sally Brown, and parishioners joined together in the celebratory procession into the congregation's own house of worship. Mother Connie acknowledged that "we have been strengthened and enlivened in our faith, and the glue of grace has blessed the community."[12]

BUILDING THE FUTURE

As the steadily growing congregation increased in membership and ministries toward financial independence, the leadership began exploring new horizons. Mother Connie described it with characteristic optimism. "The new financial maturity is only one of the many signs which continues to convince me that God wants Saint Andrew's to be a living sacrament of the impossible being accomplished not through greatness but through God's help."[13]

In February 1999, a long-term planning committee was formed. Mother Connie explained that over the next six months the committee's task will be to look prayerfully at all phases of the community's life in terms of both program and building needs and opportunities. She exclaimed, "I am excited to see what God has in store for us."[14]

Although the October 1999 fire was an unexpected detour, the intrepid visionaries continued to explore the future. Providing handicapped access to the church building and expanding the sanctuary for the growing congregation were major objectives. Preserving the almost century-old building was an imperative.

The parish prepared for its centennial celebration of its 1908 building by installing a new slate roof in 2005. The following year in 2006, the hundred-year-old windows were restored by the same premier studio that originally built them: Watkins Stained Glass Studio of Denver.

12. Lyon, "Hopes Restored," 4.
13. Delzell, "Vicar's Voice," 1.
14. Delzell, "Vicar's Voice," 2.

MOTHER CONNIE RETIRES

In 2007 Mother Connie retired from her sixteen-year ministry at St. Andrew's Episcopal Church. She began her long years of service following the restoration project of the late 1980s. She ended her St. Andrew's ministries with a vision of an expanded worship space—a major renovation to be completed in 2009 after her retirement.

In spite of Mother Connie's departure, the congregation spearheaded the major construction with tenacity and energy. Deacon Sally Brown continued to serve the parish until her retirement in October 2009, providing some clerical continuity while the parish conducted a search for their next rector. Crucial leadership was also provided by senior warden Tim Croasdaile along with Roger Kilgore, chair of the building committee. Andy Robinson and M. B. Krueger cochaired a capital campaign that raised over $900,000, exceeding their original goal of $750,000.

The structural expansion of the nave and chancel in 2008–2009 was an inspired collaboration of the congregation and its gifted lay leaders. The challenging expansion was directed by the same architectural firm that first built the church in 1908: Cram and Ferguson of Concord, Massachusetts. Ethan Anthony was the principal architect.

When the dust settled, the hundred-year-old building had been transformed. The basic design and materials originally used in 1908 were preserved or replicated. The nave was extended to accommodate more people. Seating for 88 expanded to seating for 128. The chancel was expanded to the west to include more windows. One of them was a rose window on the west wall high above the altar, designed by the Watkins Stained Glass Studio. Two side chapels now provide sculptures and prie dieux (kneelers) for private devotion. The final touch was the elevator on the north side of the building to provide handicapped access from the parking lot to all levels of the church.

In their typical and robust manner, the small congregation found multiple ways to finance the crowing jewel of their worship space. The parish had several successful capital campaigns over a three-year period. These fundraisers were matched by funds from the Colorado State Historic Fund. Additional funding came from Historic Denver. Separate funding targeted separate projects: roof, windows, and tuck pointing of brick exterior. The expansion remodeling by the Cram and Ferguson Company totaled $1.7 million. In the end, the accumulated costs resulted in a parish debt in spite of the considerable fundraising and outside support.

In 2017 the American Institute of Architects awarded Cram and Ferguson Co. their Merit Award for Design Excellence for St. Andrew's Episcopal Church in Denver. The award cited the noteworthy consistency with original architectural style and matching the exterior brick of the hundred-year-old building.

One of the longtime parishioners who joined St Andrew's in 1980 reflected on the three rebuilding projects of 1988, 2000, and 2008. She remarked, "I've done more work on the church building than my own house." A fitting tribute to a small and oftentimes struggling congregation that valued its house of worship and worked nonstop to preserve it for posterity.

A LEGACY REMEMBERED

Mother Connie's initial charge was to build up the small congregation into healthy membership and financial stability, and she did so. And then she continued to expand the leadership of the parish, which in turn expanded the ministries into uncharted territories.

Bethany House served a critical need of the 1990s by providing housing for persons dying of AIDS. The Children's Arts and Learning Center gave hundreds of inner-city children opportunities undreamed of. St. Elizabeth's School continues to nurture a thriving population of multicultural, multiracial students in the heart of Denver.

Mother Connie is a living example of the emerging equality of women in the Episcopal priesthood. In addition, she promptly assisted other women entering the clergy. For well over a decade, Mother Connie and Deacon Sally Brown co-led the seedlings of ministries at St. Andrew's. Their efforts led to local, national, and international engagement with the parish, providing financial and/ or time commitments.

Music ministry at St. Andrew's moved to another level under Mother Connie's leadership. Music in the very beginning of the parish in 1874 was valued and noteworthy. However, it was the appointment of choral director Tim Krueger along with his young St. Martin's Chamber Choir finding its headquarters at St. Andrew's that turned a corner. Maestro Krueger immediately began developing a parish choir that excelled in Anglo-Catholic musical liturgy. Choral and organ music of today's worship stands as a beacon within the city—supporting worship and providing regular concerts for the public.

Two major renovations of the church building also mark the Delzell era.

Following the disastrous 1999 fire, the church was promptly restored to beauty and function. By the ending of her ministry at St. Andrew's, Mother Connie initiated the expansion of the 1908 church building, complementing its exemplary historic stature. Restoration of artistic treasures and a meditation garden completed her legacy.

In honor of Mother Connie's legacy, the parish named a room in the undercroft as a tribute to the retiring rector. It was named the Delzell Room and is used for special meetings and serves as the choir vesting and storage room.

DOCUMENTS CONSULTED

"Arts Annex Opens Doors"
"Canon Missioner"
"Church Damaged in Blaze"
Glasier, "Looking Out"
Hendrie, letter to Olson, May 2, 1930
Historical essay, Children's Arts and Learning
Luce, "Fire in Sanctuary"
Mack, "Arts and Learning"

"St. Andrew's Awarded"

"St. Andrew's and St. John's"

Suter, letter to Fletcher, April 17, 2001

Torkelson, Religion Column

Torkelson, "Rise from Ashes"

PEOPLE CONSULTED

Ethan Anthony, principal architect, Cram and Ferguson Architects, Concord, Massachusetts

Martha Bollenbacher, parishioner, St. Andrew's Episcopal Church, Denver

Sally Brown, deacon, St. Andrew's Episcopal Church, 1995–2009

Connie Delzell, rector, St. Andrew's Episcopal Church 1991–2007

Judith James, parishioner, St. Andrew's Episcopal Church 1980–present

Michael Knudsen, administrative assistant, Bethany House, 1995–ca. 2000

Timothy Krueger, choirmaster, St. Andrew's Episcopal Church, 1995–present

Aaron Moody, Skyline Stained Glass, Denver, Colorado

Ken Near, vicar, St. Andrew's Episcopal Church, 1986–1991

Jane Watkins, Watkins Stained Glass Studio, Denver, Colorado

Epilogue

Exploring the 150-year story of St. Andrew's Episcopal Church in Denver led to unexpected discoveries. An initial revelation was the primary influence on St. Andrew's direction from nineteenth-century missionary bishop the Rt. Rev. John Franklin Spalding. Early twentieth-century influence came from the Rev. Neil Stanley's commitment to the Oxford Movement ideals which he lived out for twenty-two years at St. Andrew's Episcopal Church. Both Bishop Spalding and rector Stanley shaped the foundation of the parish's signature ministries.

Those signature ministries focused on the church's "vocation in the world"—a term coined by Lutheran theologian the Rev. Dr. Norma Cook Everist and discussed in her book *The Church as Learning Community*. In my conversation with the author (Autumn 2019), St. Andrew's work with unmet societal needs was identified: the polio epidemic, the AIDS crisis, inner-city educational needs, and stranded and ignored young people living on the streets of Denver. By establishing healthcare facilities and schools to meet these needs, the church was living out its divine purpose—its vocation in the world. Biblical mandates repeatedly direct the church to care for all people living with unmet human needs for food, shelter, clothing, or healthcare.

Following in the footsteps of Spalding and Stanley, key twentieth-century clergy provided instrumental leadership for this

147

vocational work. Exemplary lay leaders partnered with visionary clergy leaders. Together they made dual contributions to both the common good of Denver and the common good of the church.

Additional partnerships included four Episcopal religious orders working within the parish for over a century of ministries. In addition, the parish engaged in numerous partnerships with individuals and organizations beyond the institutional church.

Throughout the long history of this relatively small parish on the edge of downtown, repeated financial insufficiency led to mission status four different times. By becoming a mission of the diocese or cathedral, the parish gained additional financial support. In the fourth mission arrangement, the parish continued to engage with three significant social justice ministries. Shining through the limitations of size and financial constraints was undaunted leadership and commitment like a beacon from above.

Reflecting the scriptural foundation of this extraordinary history is the reredos above the altar of St. Andrew's Episcopal Church. Created by Denver artist Albert Byron Olson, the mural depicts five New Testament stories. The central panel is an illustration of Jesus blessing the children. Two adjacent panels represent Jesus' acts of healing and restoring life to individuals of his day. These artistic portraits anchor the worship space with affirmations of the church's "vocation in the world" as expressed in the long history of *Historic Church Serves Big City*.

The altar reredos by Albert Byron Olson was donated to St. Andrew's Episcopal Church in 1931 by Edwin Beard Hendrie. Over time, by serendipity, the reredos has come to symbolize the twentieth-century ministries of healing and education, with its three central panels depicting healing and new life along with the blessing of children.

Bibliography

Armentrout, Don S., and Robert B. Slocum, eds. *Episcopal Dictionary of the Church*. New York: Church Publishing, 2000.

"Arts Annex Opens Doors." *Open Door*, July 1993. St. John's Cathedral.

Breck, Allen D. The *Episcopal Church in Colorado: 1860–1963*. Denver: Big Mountain, 1963.

"Bishop Hill to Visit Parish." *Open Door*, November 1988. St. John's Cathedral.

"Canon Missioner." *Open Door*, June 1992. St. John's Cathedral.

Chase, Robert. "Denver Minister Says Papal Supremacy Is Only Issue." *Rocky Mountain News*, January 20, 1928

Christensen, Tito. "Father Near Answers East Coast Call." *Saint Andrew's Network*, November 1991.

"Church Consecration." *Rocky Mountain News*, September 14, 1875.

"Church Damaged in Blaze." *Denver Post*, November 1, 1999.

Cuba, Stan. *The Denver Artists Guild: Its Founding Members*. Boulder: University Press of Colorado, 2015.

Culver, Virginia. "Disparate Groups Share St. Andrew's Episcopal." *Denver Post*, October 18, 1985.

Dagwell, Benjamin. Sermon, St. John's Cathedral, Denver, January 22, 1928.

"Death Ends 26 Years Service for Fr. Stanley." *Our Church Paper*, March 1943. Colorado Episcopal Diocese.

Delzell, Connie. "Vicar's Voice." *Saint Andrew's Network*, Lent 1999.

———. "Vicar's Voice." *Saint Andrew's Network*, Advent 1999.

Everist, Norma Cook. *The Church as Learning Community*. Nashville: Abingdon, 2002.

Franklin, Cecil. *Saint Andrew's Episcopal Church*. Brochure, Spring 1985.

Glasier, Mary Grace. "Looking Out for Our Kids." *Open Door*, May 1994. St. John's Cathedral.

Bibliography

Goodstein, Phil, et al. *Historic Map of the 2000 Block of Glenarm Place*. Burbank, CA: Gotprint.com, 2017.

Grant, William W. *Such Is Life*. Denver: A. B. Hirschfeld, 1952.

Grant, William West, III. "Castlewood." Essay, Denver, April 20, 1983.

Hendrie, Edwin Beard. Letter to Albert Byron Olson, May 2, 1930.

Hodges, Eva. "Brothers Help City's Needy." *Denver Post*, November 13, 1980.

Irenaeus, Brother, ed. *Famlian*, August 10, 1975. Order of the Holy Family.

James, Judith. "Martin Near Chosen for Choir School." *Saint Andrew's Network*, October 1989.

———. "New Dean's Committee Members Named at Annual Meeting." *Saint Andrew's Network*, February/March 1990.

———. "Re-Dedication Celebrates Saint Andrew's Feast." *Saint Andrew's Network*, November/December 1988.

———. "UTO Grant Funds Center for Racial Understanding." *Saint Andrew's Network*, August 1989.

Journal of the Primary Council of the Protestant Episcopal Church in Colorado. 1918.

Kester, Phyllis, "A Transformed Life." *Colorado Episcopalian*, Advent 2016. Colorado Episcopal Diocese.

Luce, Betty, "Fire in the Sanctuary." *Historic Denver News*, March/April 2003.

Lyons, Margaret Lewis. Letter to the Rev. Connie Delzell, September 14, 2005.

Lyon, Vanessa. "Hopes Restored at St. Andrew's." *Colorado Episcopalian*, July 2000. Colorado Episcopal Diocese.

Mack, Anne. "Arts and Learning Center Reaches Children at Risk." *Open Door*, September 1995. Colorado Episcopal Diocese.

Mattingly, Terry. "Historic Parish Finds New Identity as Urban Mission." *Rocky Mountain News*, October 20, 1986.

———. "St. Andrew's Feasts on Revitalized Parish." *Rocky Mountain News*, December 3, 1988.

Michael, Brother. "Strangers in Town." *Holy Cross Quarterly* 10 (1971) 4–12.

"Mission Church of St. Andrew's." *Colorado Episcopalian*, October 1949. Colorado Episcopal Diocese.

Need, Merrie. "Sisters of St. Anne and Their Times." *Colorado Heritage* (2016) 16–23.

"Origins of St. Andrew's Episcopal Church History." In the Trinity Memorial Church parish register, 1874–1880.

"Priests Room of Chapel Dedicated to Memory of The Rev. Neil Stanley." *Colorado Episcopalian*, April 1949. Colorado Episcopal Diocese.

Raup, Eli. Letter to St. Andrew's Episcopal Mission vestry, January 7, 1920.

Schmitt, Delphine. "The Tradition of Platonic Mysticism in English Poetry." Masters thesis, University of Denver, 1934.

Stanley, Neil. "And Was Incarnate." In *Traditio Symboli*, by Neil Stanley. London: Society of SS. Peter and Paul, n.d.

———. "Apologia Mystica." In *The Pleasance of Exile*, by Neil Stanley. Unpublished, 1942.

Bibliography

————. Farewell message, St. Andrew's Episcopal Church, October 25, 1942.

————. Sermon, St. Andrew's Episcopal Church, January 22, 1928.

————. Sermon, St. Andrew's Episcopal Church, January 15, 1933.

Stark, Jon Marr. *Men Athirst for God.* Booklet, Order of the Holy Family. Denver: Abbey's Craft and Print Shop, n.d.

"St. Andrew's and St. John's Working Together." *Open Door* April 1994. St. John's Cathedral.

"St. Andrew's Awarded Safe City Grant." *Open Door*, August 1994. St. John's Cathedral.

"St. Andrew's Rector Blasts Police Raid." *Rocky Mountain News*, July 25, 1971.

Steele, Tanya. "Personality Profiles." *Saint Andrew's Network*, February/March 1990.

Suter, Erik. Letter to Kevin Fletcher, St. Cecilia Singers, invitation for Washington National Cathedral concert, April 17, 2001.

Torkelson, Jean. Religion column, *Rocky Mountain News*, June 3, 2000.

————. "Rise from Ashes." *Rocky Mountain News*, November 8, 1999.

"Tribute to Tom Titus on His Eightieth Birthday." 2004. St. Andrew's Episcopal Church archives.

White, Joyce L. *Colorado Episcopal Clergy in the Nineteenth Century: A Biographical Register.* Denver: Prairie, 2003.